Spirituality For People Who Hate Spirituality

A Primer

Also by P. Casey Arrillaga

Book

Realistic Hope: The Family Survival Guide for Facing Alcoholism and Other Addictions

Podcast

Addiction and the Family

Spirituality For People Who Hate Spirituality

A Primer

P. Casey Arrillaga, LCSW, LCDC

Recovery Tree Publishing

Spirituality for People Who Hate Spirituality: A Primer

All Rights Reserved.

Copyright © 2022 P. Casey Arrillaga

This book may not be reproduced, transmitted, or stored in whole or in part by any means, including but not limited to graphic, mechanical, or electronic without the express written consent of the author except in the case of brief quotations for reviews.

Recovery Tree Publishing
addictionandthefamily@gmail.com

ISBN: 978-1-7379815-2-7

Cover design and cover photo by P. Casey Arrillaga

Interior layout and design by P. Casey Arrillaga

Edited by Kira Arrillaga

Author photo by Kira Arrillaga

For Kira, the most spiritual atheist I know.

CONTENTS

1. Who Needs a Book on Spirituality? — 1
2. Why Is Spirituality So Important to So Many People? — 9
3. Why Is Spirituality So Hard for Some People? — 27
4. Some Common Definitions and Perspectives on Spirituality — 75
5. Making Spirituality Work for You — 91
6. Concluding Thoughts and Good Wishes — 133
7. Thanks — 135
8. References — 137

Chapter One

Who Needs a Book on Spirituality?

Nobody needs to read this book. Human beings can live, love, and thrive in the world without spirituality. To say that we don't need something, however, is not to say that we cannot benefit greatly from it. After all, people can live in a world without music, delicious food, dancing, fine arts, travel, etc. Nonetheless, our lives are greatly enriched by such things. Indeed, many people spend much of their time earning money and arranging their lives so that they can engage in these pleasures even though they don't technically need any of them.

Is spirituality just another enjoyable activity, then, one more item on the list of the good things in life? For some, the answer may be "yes" but for many people it is much more than that. They find it essential, something to guide them through their days and give them meaning. Some will see it as the most important thing about themselves, the very basis of their self-definition.

As a result, countless books have been written about spirituality, and many definitions put forward. Rather than clarify the issues, this dizzying array sometimes seems to only create more confusion.

So, who needs this book? The answer is simple. I wrote it for anyone who struggles with spirituality, loves it and wants to know more, wants ammunition to shoot it down, can't understand why it's hard for some people, finds it fascinating despite not knowing where it fits into their lives, wants to help others find it, or has been told they need it and is willing to find out if that's true. I have fit into every one of those categories at some time in my life, sometimes more than one in the same day.

Most importantly, this book is for people who hate the idea of spirituality but know that ignoring it or pushing it away hasn't gotten them where they want to be. That was me for quite a while, especially in my early recovery from addiction. I saw people who had been through the same things as me but were now thriving. They said they got there through spirituality. This didn't appeal to me much, and I was pretty sure it wouldn't work for me even if I tried, but I had run out of other ideas. If this is you too, let's talk. I think I may be able to help.

An Uncommon Definition

Despite so many people agreeing on the importance of spirituality, and so much being written about it, there is very little consensus on what that term actually means. While many definitions of spirituality have a religious component to them, an increasing number do not.

Given all this, I am going to go with the definition that I have found most helpful to me: *Spirituality is a sense of connection to something greater than yourself.* I haven't seen this definition in any dictionary. Instead, it is the product of years of grappling with how to get the benefits of spirituality in my life while not finding it easy to swallow concepts offered to me about "that which is beyond the material plane" or "the great unseen and unknown" or "that about which I feel certain just because I choose to believe it or was raised to believe it." There is plenty that I do not know or understand, and I don't claim that a lack of concrete proof means something can't be true. I've just found it hard to base my life on such things.

Since the benefits of incorporating spirituality are undeniable, I want a definition that leads to these improvements without sacrificing my values or depending on a leap of faith I am not ready to take. Thus, I go with the idea of "something greater than myself" because it is extremely broad. I'll get more into its implications later. For now, I'll just say that this openness of concept is deliberate, and it will be a running theme in this book.

My definition says "a sense of connection" rather than "a connection" because it is this sense that has been most helpful to myself and others. When I feel connected to something greater than myself, it improves my experience of life even in the face of my doubts. It no longer matters if I believe what anyone else believes, or if I am certain that I am right. This may reflect the Western tendency to value individual experience over collective belief, but it has proven to be of great practical benefit, so I'm going with it.

Therefore, when I speak of spirituality in this book, I'm talking about that sense of connection. While most definitions of spirituality will emphasize something immaterial, I have seen many people benefit greatly by defining their spirituality as a sense of connection to things that are quite observable, such as a group of fellow travelers in recovery, the beauty of nature, or the vastness of our universe. Their sense of connection may be intangible, but its object is not. Everything in this book will also work for you if you have a very abstract or vague idea of that to which you want to connect. It's okay to not have precise definitions or ideas of what it is, as long as you are willing to seek a sense of connection.

Why Me?

Earlier this morning, I listened to a friend cry halfway around the world. He felt lost and afraid, tangled up in a dilemma in which there was no clear way out. After he talked through his situation and all the emotions it stirred up in him, I offered my experience, strength, and hope as best I could. When he asked for practical advice, I kept pointing to a spiritual solution because it is the most practical thing I know.

He is a religiously observant man and I am not, yet we share a framework of looking at the world through spiritual eyes. The longer we considered his dilemma from this perspective, the more he gained insight into the causes of his problems and how to move toward solution. We ended our talk with a common prayer, he directing his words to Allah, and I to nothing I could name. We are aware of our differences, yet we have been opening and closing our talks like this for years.

Shortly thereafter, we saw each other on a daily online meeting in which people from around the world meditate together and then lift each other up in prayer and affirmation. I have never asked anyone at that meeting what they believe, but I never doubt that they believe in something. Our common goal and common good transcend any apparent differences. Reflecting on how my day has gone so far, I have to wonder how a former die-hard proselytizing atheist like myself came to this point.

The answer is simple. I need spirituality in my life. I didn't know this until I got into recovery from addiction, and even then I resisted it for as long as I could. I had been told from my first recovery meeting that spirituality was a vital component, but I was not interested. Fortunately, I couldn't stay sober on my own.

Why do I say this was fortunate? Because my inability to stay sober led me to eventually cave in and try the spiritual solution, and this has become a treasured part of my life. It not only helps me stay out of my addiction, it is also incredibly enriching, fulfilling, practical, and applies in all areas of my life.

I was inspired to write this book because I know there are many people like me, people who doubt, question, and challenge as a matter of habit, yet who could really use the benefits that spirituality offers. I am scientifically oriented by nature, so I value healthy skepticism, but I have also seen how much my life has improved through finding a spirituality that works for me. In reconciling these two things that I thought were diametrically opposed, I found myself in a position to help others do the same. This does not mean that your spirituality needs to look anything like mine. It only means that if I can find a way to make it work, so can you. I would be honored to help.

For some people, the issue is not so much skepticism as it is hurt. They cannot reconcile the pain they feel and see around them with the religious or spiritual ideas that they know. If this is you, I say that the benefits of spirituality are within your reach as well. Because it can be personal to you, spirituality can be found in a way that helps you most, regardless of what anyone else says it needs to be. You can not only find peace with your own hurt places, but also help others do the same.

Throughout this book, I draw on the experience of recovery from addiction, largely my own but at times that of people I have known on my journey. I do so because many who are trying to recover are highly motivated to seek spirituality, but of these, a good number have low trust that they can find anything that works for them. This book is by no means aimed only at such people, but I hope that some of them can find help in these pages.

I hope just as much that if you have no connection to addiction and recovery, you can also find help here. No matter what your life has been like so far, no matter what you want it to be moving forward, I invite you to experience the serenity and joy I have been so fortunate to know, through finding a spirituality that works for you.

Chapter Two

Why Is Spirituality So Important to So Many People?

While spirituality may not come easily to you or me, we cannot deny that it is vitally important to many people around the world. We could cynically write such people off as simple-minded or self-deluded, or worse yet as self-righteous and self-serving. We could say that all spiritual leaders are hucksters peddling the opiate of the masses, but honest observation shows that this is not so. Negative people may be found in any group, spiritual or not, but there are countless adherents of countless spiritual paths who are good and honest, intelligent and observant, with leaders who dedicate themselves to helping others. Many of these people will tell you that spiritualty is a central part of their lives, sometimes the basis of who they are and how they operate in the world.

What makes spirituality so important to them? To answer this question, we will look first at the nature of human happiness and how spirituality fits into it, and then we'll consider the psychological and physical benefits of spirituality. Finally, I include a special section on the benefits of spirituality for anyone recovering from addiction or any other compulsive behavior.

Happiness

Happiness is not always easy to define, let alone measure, but the growing field of positive psychology has given us tools to understand how spirituality not only fits into a deeply happy life, but can actually be its foundation.

One of the central concepts in positive psychology is that happiness has three basic forms, and that satisfaction in life involves finding a mix and balance of each.[1] One or another of these dimensions may come more naturally for you, but all are within reach.

In looking at types or forms of happiness, positive psychology splits happiness into three major categories: peak experiences, engaging experiences, and meaningful experiences.[1] Peak experiences are the stand-out moments in life, the ones that really stick with us. This may include a wedding or the birth of a child. It might be an amazing hike while traveling.[2] It could be a special meal on a special occasion. It could be a wonderful surprise as a child, a reunion with someone we never thought we would see again, or a special moment of communication with someone that stays with us for the rest of our lives.[3] We can spend a lot of time planning peak experiences but sometimes they sneak up on us. No matter how we come by them, they are an important component of happiness, and often the easiest to recognize.[1]

Spirituality offers some of the most impactful peak experiences, and many people have found that such moments have changed the course of their lives.[4] These experiences may come through the time and effort of daily dedication to deep prayer and meditation that leads to a breakthrough, such as a sudden realization that they are one with everything. Perhaps the peak experience is the result of a religious ceremony that takes years of preparation, leading to a sense of achievement and recognition that helps them define who they are from then on. Other people may come across a peak spiritual moment completely without warning, such as having a near-death experience or waking up one day to a sense that there is a divine loving presence in the room.

The most powerful are those that increase the sense of connection to something greater than themselves, whether it is a deity, an undefined source of good in their lives, or the entire universe. The deeper the sense of connection, the more powerful the experience. Many who have had such experiences say afterwards that they may have never had the precise feeling again, but that the memory of it stays with them for life, sometimes changing their sense of who they are, why they are here, how they treat others, and what they will do with the rest of their time on Earth.

Some people mistakenly think that peak experiences are the only type of happiness and can get stuck in an endless search for peak experience after peak experience. We are not built for this. In fact, our brains will acclimate to peak experiences that are repeated too often, and things that once brought great joy or excitement will become routine. Trying to beat the system by continually chasing ever more exciting moments can lead to frustration and a sense that the rest of life is dull and meaningless.

If this has been you, then it's time to acknowledge that there is more to happiness than an endless string of highs. Instead, let there be space in between the peaks, let some of them come naturally, and have gratitude when they do. Finally, let yourself recognize that there are other types of happiness as well.

Thus, we look at the second category of happiness: engaging experiences. These are the happy times that come from being engaged in things that feel both challenging and worth doing for their own sake. We seek engaging experiences not because they feel like a high, but because they help us both enjoy life and grow at the same time. Engaging experiences offer a sense of "flow" in which the time the activity requires does not seem so important. Instead, we want to savor what we are doing and feel a sense of accomplishment afterward. In other words, they are their own reward.

Peak experiences tend to lift us up quickly and often drop us back down just as quickly. Engaging experiences, on the other hand, give a gentler curve, increasing happiness over more time and sustaining it for longer. This is important because going from high to high does not lead to life satisfaction in the way that learning and growing does.

Engaging experiences do not always come easily. We may not see our progress day-to-day, and we will likely hit plateaus, but when we look back at where we started, our progress becomes clear. This allows us to engage once again and feel this level of happiness.

Common examples of engaging experiences include athletics, playing music, painting, gardening, working out, playing with children, working on a puzzle, and learning a new language. Anything that captures your attention and imagination can qualify.

Spirituality offers engaging experiences through such things as prayer and meditation practices, religious rituals, or the study of sacred or inspiring texts. Some may find spiritual engagement through walking in nature or contemplating a starry sky. Others will find it when they explore themselves or seek to emulate that which they find divine. Once again, there is no wrong answer. Instead, there is a universe of possibilities to explore. Find the things that help you create or strengthen connection to something you consider greater than yourself, and you will be on the right track.

The final category of happiness is that of meaningful experiences. These are often considered the most valuable, because without a sense of meaning, life often feels empty. This is true regardless of what else we experience, have, or accomplish. Meaningful experiences are those that involve getting beyond ourselves, often through being of service to others and to that which we consider greater than us. This might include service to those closest to us (our community), to the larger group around us (our society), to all others (our world), or to something even greater than that (our higher power). It is in getting beyond ourselves that we find the most lasting satisfaction.

In fact, it can be argued that having meaningful experiences is the best way to raise our happiness baseline, which is to say how happy we are by default. This natural happiness setting varies by person but tends to remain fairly constant no matter how their life changes.

Why Is Spirituality So Important to So Many People?

Our level of happiness may go up for a bit when something positive happens and down for a bit if something negative happens, but with time it will tend to go back to our usual. It can be lowered by long-term damage from things like addiction, unresolved grief, or trauma, but given the opportunity for healing, many people will return to their old baseline.

Is there are way to raise it and have the increase stick? There is, and it seems to be through meaningful experiences. When we engage in giving service to something greater than ourselves, we move toward such transcendent experiences. We can take on even the most difficult tasks if we find meaning in them.[5] As this happens, our overall happiness with the course of our lives tends to go up, and thus our happiness baseline is raised.

Luckily, spirituality offers a wide variety of opportunity for meaningful experiences. This is in no small part because many religions and spiritual traditions include an emphasis on being of service to others without expectation of direct or reciprocal reward. Examples include the Islamic practices of *zakat*, one of the Five Pillars of Islam, which is the obligatory giving a portion of one's wealth to help those less fortunate, and *sadaqah*, which is voluntarily giving of wealth, time, energy, kindness, etc. The other Abrahamic faiths (Christianity and Judaism) also emphasize the importance of giving and being of service. Buddhism and Hinduism both refer to selfless service as a vital part of *dharma*, which means the sacred way or law of the universe. The list goes on, but you get the idea.

Service given freely has measurable effects on our brain, most often showing up as a very rewarding activity. A number of regions are affected, especially those associated with pleasure, social connection, understanding others' emotions and needs, and the anticipation of future rewards.[6] This seems to give a neurological underpinning to the Buddhist story of the student who approaches a teacher to ask how they can serve others. The teacher replies, "What others? Serve yourself!" When the student asks how they can serve themselves, the teacher replies, "Take care of others."[7]

Physiological and Psychological Benefits

It is not only our brain that benefits from spirituality. There are also demonstratable physiological and psychological benefits, many of which overlap, so I will talk about them together and point out where each influences the other.

There has been a remarkable increase in research in about the benefits of spirituality since the late 1990's.[8] This has included many studies showing that religion and spirituality lead to longer lifespans, better recovery from illness and surgery, stronger immune response, decreased stress hormones, and lower blood pressure, among other benefits.[8] Spirituality and religion have even been found to help pregnant women sleep better, which is important because insomnia is a serious concern and a frequent complaint for pregnant women.[9]

Some studies show that spirituality, but not religiosity, can help in a small way with how chronic pain patients experience their pain, and that there is a stronger association between spirituality and better coping skills and less likelihood of such patients seeing themselves as disabled by the pain.[10] You may have caught that this last bit has more to do with the psychology of the pain rather than the pain itself. Similarly, people who are dying of kidney failure find that spirituality and religion are helpful with both their experience of physical symptoms and how much they are upset by their situation.[11] This seems to be a combination of physiological and psychological benefit.

This is reinforced by findings that show greater benefit to "intrinsic" religious practice, which is to say the aspects that feel more personal, such as prayer and meditation, rather than "extrinsic" religious aspects, which is to say those parts that are more social.[8] In other words, our inner spiritual life seems to have more of a positive influence on our health than our external spiritual life. It is not hard to imagine that this speaks to the influence of our psychology on health, something that has been clearly established by much scientific research.

With that in mind, let's look at some of the psychological benefits of spirituality. Spirituality has been found to help across a wide variety of mental health and subjective wellbeing outcomes. This includes how satisfied people feel with their lives and how well-balanced they feel between positive and negative emotions. This effect is stronger the more solid a person is in their spiritual belief.[12] Interestingly, life satisfaction seems to be positively influenced by both religious practice and non-religious spirituality, whereas the balance between positive and negative emotions is influenced more by spirituality than by religious practice.[12]

Other spiritual benefits highlighted by research include an overwhelming majority of studies showing that spiritual people are less prone to depression and suicide, with a lesser but still significant number of studies finding a reduction in anxiety.[13] An even greater percentage of scientific studies shows that more spirituality is associated with less use of alcohol and other drugs.[13] Spirituality is positively associated with psychological resilience, and seems to help people move through the challenges of aging.[14] Spirituality is also associated with making healthier choices, such as taking

HIV prevention measures when having sex.[15] Studies show that spirituality is helpful for disaster survivors.[16] Science affirms that spirituality helps people have greater hope and resilience, which in turn helps people have better physical health outcomes when they are at risk.[17] Studies show that spirituality helps people avoid loneliness and a sense of isolation.[17]

It is important to note that research has also pointed out where spirituality can be harmful to mental health. This includes findings that more rigid and controlling beliefs and religious systems can lead to guilt and shame, whether this is imposed from the outside or experienced as internal conflict.[18] Even prayer, which has been shown to have many benefits, can be problematic if a person feels they are praying to a deity who is likely to punish or abandon them.[19] Spirituality can lead to negative mental health outcomes if individuals experience real or feared rejection from their faith and/or its adherents.[18]

It is commonly thought in the scientific community that many of the physiological benefits of spirituality may in fact be a direct result of the psychological benefits. This may be visualized as a positive feedback loop, in which spirituality helps with feeling better emotionally, feeling better emotionally helps with physical health, physical wellbeing reinforces positive emotion, which in turn makes it easier to have faith in a higher power and engage in spiritual practice.

Spirituality and Addiction Recovery

It can be argued that the cascade of physical and psychological benefits of spirituality has been realized nowhere more than in the field of addiction recovery. Through seeking a spiritual solution, millions of people worldwide have reclaimed their lives, including gaining and then improving physical health, psychological wellbeing, life satisfaction, economic benefit, social connection, and a sense of purpose and meaning.[20]

The use of spirituality as a primary tool in addiction recovery is exemplified by Twelve Step recovery fellowships. Some people have referred to these fellowships as the most influential self-help movement on Earth, and they are centered squarely on the idea of a *spiritual awakening*.[21] This phrase undoubtedly signifies different things to different people. You can take it to mean anything that is helpful to get you in touch with your spiritual nature and/or a higher power. It is described in Twelve Step literature as something that can happen suddenly or slowly over time. My favorite idea is that through the process of recovery, "one's spirit awakens."

Why Is Spirituality So Important to So Many People?

Twelve Step recovery began with Alcoholics Anonymous, which was formed by people with an addiction to alcohol, many of whom had been thought of as hopeless cases, who instead found a way to save themselves from their addiction. In their basic text, *Alcoholics Anonymous*, they constantly reinforce the need for spirituality, placing repeated emphasis on the idea that "alcoholics of the hopeless variety" cannot recover without relying on a "Power greater than themselves."[22]

An amazing array of Twelve Step fellowships followed the example of Alcoholics Anonymous, each one using the same model to address a different addictive or compulsive behavior. This includes Twelve Step groups for all kinds of drugs, from specialized meetings like Crystal Meth Anonymous or Marijuana Anonymous, to the more generalized Narcotics Anonymous, which includes addiction to any drug under its umbrella. People were initially surprised that this spiritual solution worked so well on alcohol addiction, let alone that it would be equally effective for addiction to other drugs, such as heroin.

What was more surprising is that this exact same model can be successfully applied to compulsive behaviors and other issues that aren't centered on drug use. The groups Overeaters Anonymous, Self Injury Recovery Anonymous, Sex and Love Addicts Anonymous, and Gamblers

Anonymous, among others, address behavioral addictions. People suffering from more general mental health issues use the Twelve Steps in Emotions Anonymous. Twelve Step groups such as Survivors of Incest Anonymous help those who have been through traumatic experiences recover together through spirituality.

Then there are groups that are formed by and for friends and loved ones of those with an addiction or compulsive behavior. These include Al-Anon for families and friends of alcoholics, Nar-Anon for families and friends of people addicted to any drug, S-Anon for families and friends of sex addicts, etc. Adult Children of Alcoholics might qualify as both a trauma survivor group and one for those affected by someone else's addiction.

The list goes on and on of different issues that are helped through the same basic process. Each new fellowship typically changes the wording of Step One from "powerless over alcohol" to "powerless over" whatever issue is plaguing them.

In using the Twelve Steps, every one of these groups embraces a spiritual solution to their problem, even if that problem is someone else's behavior. How does that work? The idea is simple: members find healing through first admitting that they can't solve the problem by themselves (Step One), coming to believe that a higher power could help them to be okay (Step Two), and then deciding to rely on that higher power for guidance (Step Three). For the not-so-spiritually minded or outright spiritually resistant person, this may sound like an immediate no-go, but allow me to explain and it may become less of a turn-off.

First off, Alcoholics Anonymous set the tone for the whole spiritual recovery thing by establishing that every member can choose any conception of a higher power that they want. This means that while some Twelve Step groups still use the original 1930's American Protestant designations of "God" as "Him," many of the more recent Twelve Step groups take away the gender pronouns and just use the word "God" in the steps. A lot of individual members don't even say "God" when talking about their higher power, preferring to say "HP," "Bigger than Me," "the universe," or any other term that helps them connect. Many refer to their higher power as "he/she/it," or avoid the use of pronouns altogether when discussing the source of their spiritual guidance.

Members use an almost infinite variety of things as their higher power. Some turn to the religious and spiritual touchstones of their culture or upbringing. Others use ideas such as the universe, nature, the ocean, or the conception of an energy that flows through all things. Still others turn to the group of people at the meetings as their higher power, saying that they find the wisdom, guidance, support, and love that they need there. There are those who find they are better off not thinking too hard about it and simply say they have a higher power that is on their side, even if they don't have it clearly defined.

All of these people find that finding a spiritual life through those first three steps brings relief around addictive/compulsive behaviors and mental health issues, or helps them make greater peace with someone else's behaviors.

So, what do the other nine steps do? They walk the recovering person through a process that fosters a closer relationship between themselves and their higher power. Barriers to both spirituality and self-acceptance are diminished, spiritual practice and reliance are encouraged, and service is highlighted as a vital part of a fulfilled life. Through all this, the Twelve Step recovering person is promised a spiritual awakening.[22]

While spirituality in recovery is not exclusive to the Twelve Step model,[20] and is not even necessary to overcome addiction,[23] more people have recovered in Twelve Step fellowships than in any other. This may be in part due to the relative popularity of Alcoholics Anonymous over any other recovery fellowship, but no matter the reason, the benefits of spirituality for addiction recovery cannot be denied.

Why Is Spirituality So Important to So Many People?

These benefits include both protective factors, which are those things that help people avoid addiction in the first place, and curative factors, which are the things that help a person who has an addiction to get their lives back. Protective factors include religious mandates against excessive substance use or any at all, and faith communities that reinforce moderation and provide social support to cope with stressors when they might otherwise use alcohol, other drugs, or compulsive behaviors to get by.[20] The help of such protective factors is no small thing, because some people are at high genetic, psychological, and cultural risk for addiction. They need every advantage available to avoid falling prey to this deadly brain disease.

Curative factors that spirituality offers include infusion of meaning and purpose into lives that have been torn apart by addiction, a means to rebuild or replace damaged social relationships, reconnection with self and a higher power through daily spiritual practice, and both tools and a new frame of reference to cope with the trials and tribulations of life.[24]

I have witnessed these benefits happen for more people than I can count, both in my personal life and professional experience. I have also been party to these miracles and have personally gained everything I describe in this section. Spirituality has gone from something that was antithetical to my self-image to a vital part of it. I once was enslaved by my addiction and was terrified to keep it going but was more terrified to face life without it. Today, I live a life of sobriety based in spirituality instead. I see meaning in what I do and how I live. I start and end every day with prayer. I seek my higher power's will and do my best to follow it at every turn.

I do none of this perfectly, but I keep on striving to make spiritual progress because I love how it feels and how it has transformed both my external and internal experience. This is so much more than what I thought I would get when I set out to tackle my addictive and compulsive behaviors. I would have settled for cutting out a few behaviors and avoiding the consequences that were obviously coming if I didn't change. The gap between that and the amazing and fulfilling life I got cannot be put fully into words. A spiritual solution is what made it all happen.

This was not a fast or easy transition, however. In the next chapter, I talk about what makes spirituality so difficult for so many of us and offer ideas on how to overcome those obstacles so that you can have all the benefits of spirituality that I have been so blessed to enjoy.

Chapter Three

Why Is Spirituality So Hard for Some People?

Let's talk about what gets in the way of spirituality. Common problems include having too high a level of spiritual skepticism, trouble reconciling logic with spirituality, an assumption that spirituality and science are opposed, bad experiences with religion, limited thinking about what spirituality can be, fear of giving up control, feeling upset with the state of the world, depression and hopelessness, and even genetics that lean away from spirituality. As we look at each of these in turn, we will also consider how it may be addressed.

Spiritual Skepticism

Skepticism is a way of looking at the world that is based in doubt, especially doubt toward religious concepts.[1] I'll use the term spiritual skepticism for this latter concept.

Some skeptics say that they do not believe anything from certain people, particular sources, or large parts of society. In some philosophical circles, this type of categorical skepticism is known as "Cartesian skepticism" because it mirrors the debates between Descartes and his opponents.[2] General skepticism says that anything presented by others is to be examined and, when it seems especially unlikely or problematic, challenged.

This is not necessarily a bad thing. Skepticism is the basis of scientific thought and healthy skepticism is a positive trait. When taken too far, however, it can show up as closed-mindedness or even contempt for new ideas before they have been properly examined. It is this level of skepticism that most often blocks a person's attempts to find spirituality.

As you read through this section, I encourage you to notice your personal level of spiritual skepticism. Let's look at some general ideas about skepticism, and then see how you can bring your own skepticism levels into a range that will allow you to move forward on your spiritual exploration.

Skepticism is most often triggered when we are presented with ideas or "facts" that are outside of our established beliefs and general worldview. Many spiritual concepts fall into this category for a skeptical person. Such a person need not be atheist or agnostic; they may in fact have deeply held spiritual beliefs. They only need to be presented with ideas that seem too far from their own.

For instance, they may have grown up in one religion and then are told about the beliefs of another. The more unfamiliar these ideas, the more skeptical the person is likely to be. Our skeptic will probably not be swayed by how many people share the new-sounding beliefs; they just know that what they are hearing seems improbable. For as long as different cultures have crossed paths, such skepticism has been present.

Spiritual skeptics of this type usually miss the fact that their own beliefs are to some extent a result of happenstance. If they had been born at another time, in another place, to a different family, etc., then their deeply-held beliefs might simply match those circumstances instead, and thus be completely different. They often do not see that they could just as easily be skeptical of the ideas they now treasure.

I don't point this out to criticize what they believe or how strongly they believe it. Instead, I hope to encourage a humility that <u>reduces unfounded skepticism and increases open-mindedness</u>.

An even stronger skepticism about different or unfamiliar spiritual concepts can occur in someone who did not grow up with their present beliefs, but instead chose them later in life. People who do this may transcend skepticism and become openly resistant to spiritual ideas that do not match their own. Such people may have grown up in one religion but chose another, have had no faith but found one later, or have been raised with a religion but chose atheism or agnosticism instead.

In such cases, I make an even stronger call for humility. When someone once believed differently than they do, perhaps with equal intensity, they might do well to be understanding when others do not flock to their newfound ideas. Unfortunately, since the new faith feels so strong, many such people go in the opposite direction by insisting that others follow them to the new light. For those around them, I encourage patience, and hope such fervor cools over time.

Any of these scenarios seems more likely to happen while moving through adolescence, which can begin as early as 8 years old and is not over until about age 25. This essential phase of development includes an inherent need for differentiation from the family and concurrent willingness to challenge the establishment. It is also an age in which new ideas are presented or noticed for the first time, and these ideas will often be more interesting than at any other life stage. Adolescence seems to be custom-made for taking greater risks in hopes of greater rewards. Few things can seem as risky or rewarding as trying a new spiritual path, with its fresh take on the world, promises of spiritual and earthly benefits, and ability to really upset the people who raised you.

At this life stage, many people either take on a Cartesian skepticism about anything associated with religion or become stauncher in defending the beliefs with which they were raised. If they become disenchanted with their childhood beliefs, it can lead to skepticism that extends far beyond the spiritual realm.

Of course, some people become spiritual skeptics much earlier in life. I certainly did. I grew up being taken to religious services but didn't see what they had to do with me. I mostly tuned out anything said in the children's spiritual instruction. However, as I grew into adolescence, I always found religious people interesting. I enjoyed debating with them, and even dating them, but never seriously considered anything their religions had to offer. I just enjoyed arguing.

I did try setting my spiritual skepticism aside by diving into religion headfirst for about six months when I was in college. At first, I attended the "college church" with its rock band and young attendees who turned out to be sleeping with each other. I grew disenchanted with the apparent hypocrisy and so I joined a sect so strict that it refused to give itself a name. We had adherents who rented things rather than buying them, ostensibly due to their faith that the new kingdom would be ushered in at any moment. I did my best to fit in, but skepticism still lurked in my heart.

One day as I was questioning whether I really subscribed to anything I was trying so hard to believe, my roommate announced that his rock band was playing at a club that night and that my other roommate's girlfriend would be entering the wet t-shirt contest. I wasn't doing drugs at the time, but it turns out sex and rock and roll were enough to end my run at being a religious person.

After I got married, I welcomed those who rang our doorbell to proselytize, and my wife would roll her eyes and wander off as I cheerily engaged in a dynamic back-and-forth with the religious adherents. My skepticism of their ideas never wavered any more than their skepticism about mine. As you may imagine, these conversations did nothing to advance my spiritual development because my renewed skepticism of anything religious simply ran too deep.

When I first started into recovery from addiction, I carried this same spiritual skepticism. It got in the way of trying the spiritual tools of the recovery fellowship I was attending. I nonetheless took what I could from the rest of the program. Trouble was, I didn't stay continuously sober this way. After enough pain and frustration, I tried the spiritual ideas and practices despite my habitual skepticism. I felt foolish doing things like prayer and meditation, but I also felt foolish showing up at yet another meeting saying I was starting my sobriety clock over again. Eventually, the fact that I was getting results from spirituality was undeniable and so my spiritual skepticism diminished. That doesn't mean it was easy, but I found it was increasingly possible.

Everyone has some level of skepticism. Those who seem too skeptical may be labeled unreasonable, overly suspicious, or even paranoid. Those who don't seem skeptical enough may be called naïve, gullible, or even "sheep" who just go along with whatever they are told. Of course, what qualifies as "too skeptical" or "not skeptical enough" is usually measured against one's own level of skepticism.

How a person arrives at their inherent level of skepticism may be influenced by many factors. Leading skepticism researcher R. Kathy Hurtt calls inherent skepticism *trait skepticism* and points to six major traits: a questioning attitude, withholding of judgment until there is sufficient evidence, curiosity, taking others' motives into account, and having faith in one's own judgment rather than assuming others are trustworthy or correct.[3]

The level of skepticism in a given situation or towards a given claim will be a combination of trait skepticism and what Hurtt calls *state skepticism*, which is skepticism that is generated or diminished by circumstances. We might say that the combination of trait skepticism and state skepticism will create a *skepticism quotient* that varies by situation, mood, etc. Here's where Cartesian skepticism comes in. If you tend to categorize all things religious or spiritual as worthy of skepticism and already have a high level of trait skepticism, then any religious or spiritual concept will have a high barrier to overcome. In other words, your skepticism quotient will be too high to even keep an open mind, and doubt will consistently overcome faith. [OR]

If this is the case for you but you want to at least explore spiritual options, what can you do? First of all, consider how much of your skepticism quotient is trait skepticism and how much is state skepticism. Are you a person with average skepticism in general who is very skeptical of spiritual ideas, or are you someone who is highly skeptical in general and spirituality just feels a little more improbable than most other things?

The answer to such questions will help determine your approach to gaining a more spiritually open mind. If you are someone who has average skepticism in general but finds you apply a strong Cartesian skepticism to spirituality, you might look for and start to address the reasons why spiritual matters get such a bad rap in your book.

When you discount or discard spiritual ideas, do you associate all of them with your objections to a particular faith or religious tradition? It has been observed that most atheists think they have strongly-held objections to all religions but really have strongly-held objections to a particular religion or family of religions, and in fact have scant knowledge of the breadth of human spiritual belief.[2] They usually have a bone to pick with whatever religious ideas were presented to them as children or are dominant in the culture in which they live. Most have not taken the time to explore the incredibly wide range of beliefs out there.

It would be almost impossible to know all of the spiritual options, but seeing how many different ideas are out there may help you move away from lumping all spiritual belief into one box that you then put in the trash. Instead, consider that there are so many forms of spirituality available that you may be able to find one you like or develop one of your own. At the very least, the plethora of spiritual ideas justifies keeping an open mind.

Ignorance of the variety of spiritual options is not the only reason people have Cartesian skepticism about all spirituality. We may be especially skeptical when ideas have implications that seem problematic. For many spiritual skeptics, this is a major barrier to belief.

For instance, some religions present the idea of an omnipresent, omnipotent, and omnibenevolent deity. The contrast between this description and the widespread cruelty and suffering seen in the world may lead even a moderately skeptical person to reject all spirituality. Some argue that they cannot accept the idea of a deity that has lower moral standards than they do. The skeptic observes that if they had the power to eradicate suffering, they would do so without hesitation, yet the deities presented do not.

To such skeptics, I say that there are many spiritual paths that do not rely on a deity, let alone one whose qualities seem to clash with observable reality. Even spirituality that is based in a higher power does not need to have a deity as you may think of it. In Chapter Five, I give practical suggestions about how to make this work for you.

Another idea that leads to Cartesian skepticism about spirituality is that there are unseen forces beyond our control that influence our lives. This is especially troubling for people who don't like the way their lives are going or have powerful negative feelings about the state of the world. This can lead to a visceral reaction to spiritual concepts that goes far beyond any intellectual objections. It can also lead to the belief that the skeptic should not trust anything outside of themselves.

Such reactions are most likely to be found among people who have had bad experiences with authority, such as those who have lived under an oppressive government or been subject to community prejudice. It especially strong in people who had trauma as children, especially at the hands of those who were supposed to care for them.

Why Is Spirituality So Hard for Some People?

This was definitely true for me. Those who raised me all had good intentions that were thwarted by their own issues. This led to a childhood that was a mix of love, support, kindness, fun, emotional disconnection, terror, violence, and abuse, all from the people on whom my life depended: my primary caregivers. Like most kids in such a dilemma, I had to come up with something to feel safe.

In my toddler and early childhood years, this involved stuffing my feelings while making plays for my parents' attention, doing nice things for them, or simply obeying their commands. Due to my emotional distress, this was hard to keep up, and I would act out or tune out, often disconnecting from everyone around me. I've been told that even as a toddler, I would run as fast as I could down the aisles of a store without looking back. Most kids want to know where their parents are for reference and safety. I was apparently not concerned with this, perhaps because I was already skeptical about reliance on anyone. My adoption at two-and-a-half sealed the deal. I felt certain I was on my own and operated accordingly.

As I reflect on this, I see many parallels between my life experiences and my struggle with spirituality. A lot of religious traditions present a deity or set of deities that are every bit as capricious as my parents seemed to be. Some, such as Greek, Roman, or Hindu cosmologies, describe their deities as having human foibles but divine abilities, which can make for a dangerous or beneficial mix, depending on how they show up that day and whether the humans involved have curried their favor. Sometimes one god lashes out at another, yet it's humans who bear the brunt or are treated like pawns. Other spiritual traditions, such as many Christian sects, describe their deity as loving of all yet also willing to condemn people to everlasting torture for believing or doing the wrong thing.

Many children have undergone these same conditions, getting punishment or favor from their parents for reasons they can scarcely guess. For those who grew up in a home in which love and danger came from the same parent, the religious descriptions may feel all too familiar and even seem repulsive. Under such conditions, it is no wonder that some of them grow skeptical of the religious ideas with which they are presented.

This can be made worse if those ideas come from the same caregivers or other authority figures who seem threatening. People who have been through this often need to heal their emotional wounds before they can sufficiently embrace a spirituality that works for them.

In my own journey, I found that therapy helped immensely with this. I did not go into it with the intention of creating a closer spiritual bond. Instead, this became an

Why Is Spirituality So Hard for Some People?

unexpected but welcome benefit. As I reduced the pain, self-pity, self-justification, and anger in my life, it became easier to see how spirituality could benefit me and how I might accept it. As I turned the volume down on my fears, especially fears around abandonment and control, I was more able to accept that I did not need to figure everything out, accurately predict the future, or be in control of everything in order to be safe. I still need to remind myself of these truths on a regular basis, but emotional healing has made it much easier, and spirituality has become a powerful tool to help with that healing.

Working on past trauma, especially abuse, was the most helpful with all of this. Doing this work allowed me to see that I had support all along, and that it was safe to acknowledge and accept it. It also left me less skeptical when circumstances didn't specifically warrant it. This was partly because I relaxed in my old pattern of having to be right all the time and had a much better understanding that I can be okay no matter what happens. I also came to feel less fear in my day-to-day life. These changes in my thinking created room for spiritualty, which in turn reinforced the new thinking. This created an upward spiral that I continue to travel today. Such therapeutic and spiritual growth is not an event. Instead, it is a process and an experience, one that I highly recommend.

Problems With Logic in Relation to Spirituality

Spirituality and logic are not necessarily opposed, but they are not best friends, either. Spirituality often is thought of as defying or transcending logic. For some people this is part of its appeal, but many others cite it as a major roadblock on their spiritual path.

For those in this second group, anything that defies or sidesteps logic is suspect. This is because so many illogical things turn out to be incorrect. In the case of religious and spiritual concepts, illogical ideas may be well-meaning but misguided. This might be forgiven, but it doesn't encourage belief.

To make things worse, illogical spiritual ideas are all too often deliberate attempts to fool people into giving up freedom, money, power, etc. Seeing such things happen, let alone having them personally attempted on you, is a powerful deterrent to accepting any spiritual idea that doesn't make logical sense.

Spiritual proponents may tell you to set logic aside and just go with the experience. Some religious sects have gone so far as to declare that logic and reason are inherently bad, associated with worldly desires rather than the higher matters with which spirituality concerns itself.[4] This is not a convincing argument for a logic-minded person, especially one who is wary of being fooled. They may see many around them try it but still are not excited about taking that plunge.

Some spiritual proponents attempt to make their spiritual ideas fit a logical framework. Such attempts are usually tortuous and fall apart when examined too closely. Contradictions abound and there is always a leap of faith that must be taken. Those of us who don't like taking such leaps without a good reason, especially when the landing place seems uncertain, are more likely to stand aside with our arms crossed and keep poking holes in what is being suggested.

This was my approach. I felt confident debating with people of faith because I sensed that they were at a disadvantage. Debate is often centered on logic, and spirituality is not inherently logical. This is not its appeal to those who embrace it, yet our society reveres logic and often touts it as the gold standard for making decisions. Thus, adherents of faith feel obligated to talk about why their beliefs make logical sense even when they clearly don't. When debating, I could wait for them to fall into any number of logical traps and then pounce.

Taking into account that I carried many of the psychological reasons for skepticism given in the previous section, it is no wonder that I cited its lack of logic as a good reason to reject spirituality altogether. If this is true for you also, I'll ask you to have patience and hear me out about some reasons to consider it anyway.

I thought of people who were spiritual as being willing to abandon logic in return for… what? A sense of security even when they knew their beliefs were not true? Loyalty to that with which they were raised? A chance to feel that they had found an answer the rest of us lacked? None of these did it for me, but I now know that many people embrace spirituality for reasons other than these. They may set their logic, or more accurately their skepticism, aside because spirituality gives them something that logic cannot.

Indeed, spirituality is perhaps best understood as fulfilling human needs that are quite different that those that logic provides. First and foremost is that human experiences of fulfillment, happiness, contentment, transcendence, and meaning cannot be found with logic alone, yet they are vital parts of a full life. In fact, without these things, life often feels empty and leaves people going from one day to the next wondering why they bother to get up in the morning. They may feel restless because something is always missing, no matter what they do or get. While advertising tells you that spending more money on products and services will take care of this, I can save you a lot of time and resources by stating the obvious: it won't.

Why Is Spirituality So Hard for Some People?

This is because we need transcendent experiences to have a life that feels worth living. These may be singular and spectacular moments, but are more likely to be small, repeated times of feeling especially connected. The more of these we store up, the better we feel about ourselves and our lives.

Thus, there is a logic to embracing faith, but it is not found by trying to make faith logical. This is likely because spirituality and logic rely on different parts of our brain. Our spiritual experiences primarily use the temporal lobes and associated structures[5], whereas logic relies on the frontal lobe. Thus, when we have a spiritual experience, we are not primarily using the logical part of our brain. Instead, we are more likely to be focused on connection, getting outside of ourselves, feeling the presence of the divine, letting go of ego, having unusual sensory experiences, and being open to ritual and authority beyond ourselves.[6] Each of these things can be an important and powerful part of our lives, and each enlists different brain structures than the ones we use for logic.

This means that a person who relies on logic as their sole guiding principle will likely need to make room for some less-logical things in their lives. This may come through deliberate efforts to quiet this part of the mind and see what else is out there. It may come through facing and quelling the fears that lead to relying solely on logic as a guardian. By easing those fears, we can allow other parts of the brain to have more of a say.

I did this through therapy and making myself try spiritual practices even when they didn't seem logical enough for my skeptical mind. I had to stick with them until I started to see the beneficial effects. I am very glad that I did.

Spirituality vs. Science

Many people assume that spirituality and science are natural enemies. This is reinforced by historical conflicts between them and also by modern rhetoric on both sides. As illustrated in the previous section, however, science and spirituality each have a place in our lives and need not be seen as an either/or choice.

In fact, spirituality has been studied extensively by science, with many affirming results, and adherents of spirituality have often been on the forefront of scientific inquiry and discovery. As detailed in Chapter Two, science proves that spirituality benefits both physical and mental health. To briefly summarize here, scientists have shown that spirituality improves everything from mortality rates to blood pressure, from stress hormones to pregnant mothers' sleep, and from depression and anxiety to a sense of overall satisfaction with life. While there are many more examples, this should be enough to show that science is not out to get spirituality, and in fact often helps make the case for spirituality's benefits. Science has also been clear about where religious belief can be a detriment to mental health, such as when a person feels that their faith condemns them, or that a given spiritual community will turn against them.

Unfortunately, it is sometimes these very same rigid spiritual belief systems or religions that have the biggest beef with science. This seems to be a result of thinking that new knowledge and the questioning of established beliefs is dangerous. This flies in the face of the philosophy of science, which says that all knowledge is up for question. In addition, science is based in a belief that logical conclusions drawn from observable facts are the gold standard, and that anecdotal evidence is not to be trusted if it does not match with commonly observed or reproducible results. If a system of spiritual belief is based on the idea of, "You should believe this because I tell you so," then its adherents may not be happy when someone replies, "I need observable proof before I will believe." Worse yet, scientific experiment may prove that the spiritual ideas being offered are wrong.

History has some quite famous stories of religious adherents threatening or even killing scientists who question their beliefs. Going to lesser extremes, religious people have challenged the teaching of scientific knowledge in schools when it contradicts the tenets of their faith. Coming from the other direction, some scientists have gone out of their way to criticize spirituality and make fun of believers. It is such things that lead people to think that science and spirituality are enemies. As with so many controversies, this is really driven by a small proportion of the people on either side.

Most people are perfectly happy to tolerate those who believe differently. Religious people use the fruits of scientific advancement every day and don't see a conflict. Many scientists around the world consider themselves religious, with between 10% (US and UK) and 66% (Turkey) in a recent survey saying that they have no doubt that God exists.[7] Perhaps more importantly, the dominant view among all the scientists surveyed was that science and spirituality have no conflict because they deal with different aspects of the human experience and answer different questions about life.[7]

It is this last idea that may help you most. As we saw in the section on logic, spirituality harnesses different parts of the brain. Thus, science can tell us how we experience spirituality but does not inherently create it for us. If we see spirituality as a separate need in our lives, then science only reinforces the idea that it is highly beneficial.

For instance, science shows that the benefits of prayer and meditation are equally available through the spiritual practices of different faiths, whether it is the personal prayer of Protestant Christianity,[8] the codified daily ritual prayer of the Muslim *salat*,[9] various mindfulness meditations from Hindu and Buddhist faiths,[10] or the non-religious but spiritual practice of Japanese Shinrin-Yoku (*forest bathing*).[10]

Can science offer anything to enhance spirituality besides telling us which parts of the brain respond to it and how they benefit? I believe it can. For me, the scientific method provided a familiar and safe framework in which to learn more about what works for me spiritually. I did this by following the basic steps of the scientific method:

1. Ask a question.
2. Do background research.
3. Form a hypothesis.
4. Design or replicate an experiment that tests the hypothesis.
5. Draw a conclusion.
    a. If the hypothesis is supported only partly or not at all, do one or more of the following:
        i. Ask a new question.
        ii. Form a new hypothesis.
        iii. Find a more accurate hypothesis.
    b. If the hypothesis is strongly supported, move forward.
6. No matter your results, communicate what you have learned and compare with what other researchers have found.

Here's how I applied this to my budding spirituality:

1. *Ask a question* – My basic question was whether prayer could help me.

2. *Do background research* – There is an abundance of literature about prayer, written in many languages, from many faiths, over thousands of years, saying that prayer is beneficial. A survey of modern scientific literature confirms this to be true. The method of prayer seems less important than the fact that prayer of some sort happens. As mentioned earlier, the only time prayer seems to lose its benefit and might become a hindrance is when the person praying believes they are praying to someone or something that judges, rejects, or might harm them. All of this encouraged me to pray in a way that felt comfortable, or at least tolerable, and to set my intention to pray to only that which might be helpful to me.

3. *Form a hypothesis* – This was trickier than I originally thought. My temptation was to hypothesize that there is a higher power that is there to help me. The problem with this is that a good scientific hypothesis is one that you can demonstrate with a good bit of certainty. If people could prove beyond a shadow of a doubt that their higher power exists, then the spiritual landscape would be a lot different.

Some people claim to have proof, but it's usually pretty subjective and can get outright self-centered at times. For instance, someone might say, "I know there is a god who loves me because I survived a terrible car accident." Outside of the fact that one can presumably survive a terrible car accident through other means, including chance and physics, this idea doesn't seem to take into account all the people who died in similar accidents. Do they not have a god? If they do, does that god not love them? The implications of this do not sit well with me.

Thus, I needed a more concrete and provable hypothesis. I found one through re-examining my original question. I wasn't trying to see if there really is a higher power that is there for me. I was asking if prayer itself could help me. Based on the existing research, it was not a big leap to form my hypothesis: **Prayer can help me, even if I'm not certain that there is anything listening.**

4. *Design or replicate an experiment that tests the hypothesis* – This part was not too tricky. I will never know who first came up with this experiment, but it was simple and a classic: **Pray.** The only hard part about it was overcoming my prejudice about prayer and those who practiced it. Luckily, my experiment would yield useful results even if I had no faith. In fact, I could learn a lot because I had a hypothesis that included my doubt.

I knew that the more data one gathers in an experiment, the more likely that accurate results will be generated, especially results that can be applied in different situations. Thus, I began praying at least once a day, and figured I would keep it up until I either saw some results or could not go on with this "useless" activity anymore.

As you may have guessed, I saw results long before I had given up. I don't remember how long it took, but I started to feel a little better as prayer became part of my routine. I thus increased the pace of my research by praying both in the morning and at night, and then I incorporated it more and more throughout my day. The longer I continued my experiment, the better I felt for doing it.

5. *Draw a conclusion* – This was the easiest part of the process. It was very obvious to me that prayer was helping.

6. *No matter your results, communicate what you have learned and compare with what other researchers have found* – For this stage, I could talk with others in my circle, especially those that had tried this experiment. While most of them would not frame it as scientific research, they all drew the same conclusion: prayer helps them. This also matched the majority of scientific literature.

I saw that when people are dissatisfied with prayer, it seems to be the result of asking for certain outcomes but not getting them. This led me to avoid this type of prayer, and instead to pray for guidance and a good attitude. This helped me refine my conclusion to the following: **Prayer helps me, even if I'm not sure there is anything listening, as long as I only pray to that which is helpful, and I ask for guidance and a good attitude rather than for my preferred outcomes.**

I should note that as I continued the prayer experiment, I grew more comfortable with the idea that something might be listening and perhaps even helping. I also had a lot of internal debate about just what that was, often changing my mind several times each day about the identity of my higher power. While this didn't interfere with my experiment, it didn't do much for my peace of mind.

Eventually, I came to see that reason I wanted to define my higher power was that I thought understanding would make me safer. This is great when it comes to science and logic, but since I am feeding a different part of my brain, understanding is not as necessary. I thus concluded that I don't need to define my higher power. I just need to keep taking the action that is helping me: regular prayer in which I ask for guidance from whatever is helpful to me.

Bad Experiences With Religion

Bad experiences with religion can present a strong barrier to spirituality, but I have seen many people overcome this. If this is an issue you face, take hope. It may take time and practice, but the results are well worth the effort.

What qualifies as a bad experience with religion? This could be one moment or event that really rocks someone's world, such as the loss of a loved one to a sudden and/or painful end despite years of faith or fervent prayers for their life to be spared, but most bad experiences happen over the long-term. They come from repeated experiences with religion that inspire fear or distaste. This might be due to threats, prejudice, discord with a person's core values, or anything else that provokes strong negative emotions.

For example, fear might have come through being threatened as a child that you would be punished by a god or gods if you did not behave in the ways your caregivers wanted. The more often this was repeated, the greater the fear may have grown. If those same caregivers punished you themselves, this may have modeled that authority figures would inflict emotional or physical pain if they were disobeyed, or worse yet, if they were angry. It would be easy for a child to believe that if their caregiver can treat them this way, then a deity might easily do the same. This could be reinforced if the religion talked about that deity in parental terms, such as referring to the deity as "Our Father" or "The Divine Mother."

Even greater fear may have come through being threatened not only with immediate punishment, but that there would be indefinite consequences if you did not obey or believe as your caregivers or religious leaders wanted. Examples of this might include threats that if you didn't believe what is being taught or do things right then you would be reincarnated into a worse life, or you would spend eternity being physically and psychologically tortured. If taken seriously, such threats can be terrifying, and children can become emotionally scarred by repeatedly being terrorized.

While I did not grow up with that fear, I have done therapy with several clients who found that these threats helped define their view of themselves and the world. Some were conflicted as adults, not sure if they could fully believe that a higher power would threaten them like this but also uncertain about fully letting their guard down. Others have rejected all religion as a result, making it very hard for them to connect with any spirituality despite wanting that sense of connection and support.

Some families punish or threaten to abandon a family member who doesn't believe what the rest of the family believes, becomes romantically involved with someone of the "wrong" faith, or otherwise steps too far out of line with the family or community's religion. Some spiritual traditions actually recommend or even demand this. For those raised in such a faith, the threat of this happening may be ever-present, which is likely to create anxiety and resentment.

I have worked with people who have suffered this fate. They talk about the anger and fear that came from being cast out of the only community they had known. Some have seen their family divided due to being exiled from their faith. For such people, gaining any sense of spirituality can be very difficult. Some have abandoned it altogether while others have tried to make their way back to the faith of their childhood. For many of them, it seems difficult to find a middle path.

This highlights the prejudices found in some religions. Most common is the prejudice that "people of our faith are better than others." This prejudice could be mild but is sometimes very strong, to the point that people who do not share the religion are considered lesser than "the chosen few." Sometimes religions also encourage prejudice against types or classes of people in a society, or those who act against the moral codes of the religion.

For instance, some religions have codes against having sexual or romantic relationships with people who were assigned the same gender at birth. If someone raised in such as faith finds themselves being attracted to others of the "wrong" gender, there can be a lot of emotional discord based in fear of being outcast by their peers, family, religious community, etc. They may fear for their lives. These concerns may be realistic or they may be the result of years of exaggeration by authority figures who were attempting to discourage homosexual behavior. It may be a mix of both. Regardless, what is important is that the fears feel realistic to the person who is stepping out of line from their religious tradition. Perhaps most psychologically destructive is the self-condemnation that can result, whether anyone else knows of the attractions or not.

Similar prejudice may come up if a member of one religion falls in love with someone of a rival religion. Individually and collectively, the couple may face anything from getting the cold shoulder to receiving death threats. Some may be the victims of violence to property or person. Their children may also run into social problems, possibly getting prejudice or pressure to pick one side or the other within the family.

A religious person can also experience prejudice that does not come from the members of the religion itself, but instead from the larger society if their religion is one that is viewed unfavorably. For instance, a Muslim in a majority Christian or Hindu community may find themselves the victim of many types of prejudice. While some may find this strengthens their faith and binds them together with others of their same religion, others may find themselves turned off by the whole thing. Abandonment and even hostility toward any type of religion or spirituality may result.

Some of the bad experiences around prejudice and religion don't have to directly involve the person at all. It can be enough to see this prejudice happen to a friend, a loved one, others in a community, or just to hear about it in the news. People may feel disappointment or disgust in hearing about a religious crusade or act of terrorism that left thousands dead, injured, or orphaned, seeing a religious leader call for hateful attitudes or acts against certain groups of people, hearing non-believers or a minority group blamed for the ills of the world, or the more personal stories of a friend being rejected by their family for religious differences. Any of these can lead a person to turn their back on all religion or spirituality.

Discord with a person's core values can happen through such experiences, but this is not the only way. Such discord can also occur when vital values such as fairness, teamwork, love of learning, or forgiveness seem to be discarded in the name of religion. Worse yet is when a given religion gives lip service to such values, but its actual practices seem to violate them. In fact, the hypocrisy of this can be a violation of core values all by itself.

For instance, I have seen religious people in my society favor others of their same religion when giving out charity despite preaching fairness and mercy toward all. When this happens, I have felt pushed away from that religion. Other times, I have heard religious adherents say directly that curiosity and love of learning should be discouraged unless applied only to study of their religion. Some have said all learning beyond strictly prescribed roles should be discouraged among women. This has turned me away from religion even if in doing so I have painted with too broad a brush.

Other things that provoke strong negative emotions towards religion and spirituality might include anything from religious wars and crusades to having people regularly attempt to proselytize to them. I remember when my daughter read a library book that had depictions of the Christian crusades in Europe. She was horrified at the imagery of people who shared the same faith as some of her closest friends slaughtering people who did not share their religion. It took a while for me to realize that she had started to wonder if her friends and their families would rise up one day and kill us. I reassured her that these events were long past, but I knew that in some parts of the world today, such things still happen. The weaponry of war has become more efficient, but the spirit is still the same. While my daughter eventually found a spiritual path that suited her, this sort of thing definitely did not help.

How can a person who wants spirituality find it despite bad experiences with religion? This simplest starting point is to realize that spirituality can be found separately and distinctly from religion. That is to say, a sense of connection to something greater than yourself is not dependent on a given set of rituals and rules. For those raised in a particular faith or society that takes for granted that one religious text or teaching is the "divine word," it may be difficult to conceive of independent spirituality. Difficult is not the same as impossible, however, and this is an area in which the effort is well worth it.

Some people find it helpful to explore how many religious and spiritual paths are out there. They may be looking for something that fits better than what they know, or they may find it helpful to open their minds to the infinite possibilities of spiritual thought without needing to take on anyone else's beliefs.

Some stay with their religion, but find it helpful to recognize that each adherent of that religion has their own beliefs. They may take a common vow and chant or sing in unison, yet if each person was interviewed in depth, it would become apparent that every one of them focuses on different parts of the belief system, has their own favorite part of the common prayer, has other parts of the religion that they acknowledge but do not emphasize, and may have things in the religion that they question or ignore. This means that whether they mean to or not, everyone chooses what they believe. For some, this is a conscious choice and for others it is unconscious. Once you see this, you can make your own conscious choice about what your religion will mean to you.

Similarly, it can help to acknowledge that since a religion is made up of many people who all have their own beliefs, the prejudices of some adherents do not necessarily speak for all. It can be painful or frustrating to encounter such prejudice but that doesn't mean that you have to give up on all people of that faith, let alone give up on spirituality altogether.

If you find yourself taking on self-condemnation as a result of the prejudice, then I urge you to let that go. This can be done through affirmations, exploring your own beliefs, engaging in positive spiritual practice, talking with supportive people, and therapy.

Through all of this, always remember that you can and will believe what you choose to. You can have a rich spiritual life within or without religion. Free your mind from internal prejudice, including prejudice for or against religion, and let yourself have the spiritual experience you deserve.

Limited Thinking About Spirituality

It turns out that limited thinking about spirituality is the Achilles heel of many atheist arguments.[11] This is because most atheists seem to have a bone to pick with one or more of the major world religions, most often the one that is prevalent in their culture. I can't blame them for not knowing all the vast number of religious ideas currently available, let alone the unfathomable number of religions that have been believed and practiced throughout history. Who could? Nonetheless, I have to keep this in mind when someone says they are against spirituality, because their thinking about spirituality is probably based in a false equivalency between religion and spirituality, and their arguments against religion are likely limited to the one(s) with which they are most familiar.

Some use the plethora of religious ideas to say that all spirituality is wrong. After all, doesn't the fact that so many people have believed so many things show that it is all just made up, and somewhat arbitrarily at that? Perhaps, but it may instead show that spirituality is best left up to the individual. As I argue in the previous section, to a great extent this happens whether people intend it or not, so I advocate for embracing this reality and letting each person choose what they will believe.

When I unchained my spirituality from anyone else's beliefs, I freed myself to believe what worked best for me. I was then able to most fully put the scientific process outlined above into practice. I didn't have to worry about proving or disproving anyone else's ideas. I didn't need to have a fully formed philosophical or religious system. I just had to allow myself to be open-minded and to have whatever experience I had without judgment. To paraphrase one of the addiction recovery fellowships, I didn't have to say "yes" to spirituality, I just had to stop saying "no."

Fear of Giving Up Control

In both my work with others and in my own life, I have come to see that when we like to be in control, it usually means that we don't feel safe otherwise. This may stem from childhood experiences in which we felt little sense of power when we got hurt physically, psychologically, or sexually. It may also come from times when we felt like our needs were not being met and we had no power to change this. The greater the frequency and severity of such things, the more profound the effect. Some of us developed a tendency to give our power over as a result, but many others developed a desire to be in control.

For me, this process started with some of my earliest experiences. My first memory involves nursing with my birth mother in the first three months of life. I remember feeling that I had to keep her attention for as long as possible and get as much as I could as fast as I could. She has confirmed that this is valid, as she only felt connected to me when we were nursing. This means that for most of the time in those early days of life, I likely sensed that I was not getting what I needed. Even at such an early age, the idea of keeping my mother's attention felt like survival. This was the beginning of my desire for control.

As I grew, I ran into more and more situations that felt dangerous, some justifiably so. In the first few years of my life, I was threatened or hurt physically, sexually, and psychologically. Some of this was intentional and much was not, but as a child I could not distinguish. Each such experience reinforced the idea that I would be better off in control.

When I was introduced to religious concepts, I was not particularly interested. The idea of a god meant less control left for me. I thought the authority figures in my life weren't to be trusted, so a higher power who was the ultimate authority figure was not an appealing concept.

I might have continued like this for life if I hadn't had a few key experiences. One big one was that I fell in love with and married a young woman who convinced me to go to therapy with her. Through this, I processed some of those early experiences and lessened the fears that stemmed from them. This didn't make me into a spiritual person, but it helped remove barriers to future exploration.

The next big experience was that I entered recovery from addiction and was told that spirituality would be key in maintaining sobriety. I was not excited or particularly open to this, but a few relapses changed my mind. My childhood fears still told me I shouldn't give up control, but I saw that I was not doing a great job of running things. This left me more and more willing to try the spiritual ideas that seemed to work so well for others. Luckily, the recovery fellowship that I had embraced had a very open idea of spirituality, one in which each person was completely free to choose their own idea of a higher power. While some of the literature of the fellowship used terms borrowed from Christianity, such as referring to "God," I was repeatedly told not to let the language get in the way. Since I could choose my own conception of a higher power, I was able to come up with something that I wouldn't mind running my life.

I found it helpful to write out a list of the qualities I wanted in that higher power. I started with things like *loving*, *caring*, and *personal*. As time went along, I thought of new qualities that I wanted or needed, so I added them to the list. If you want to see my current list, it can be found in Chapter Five. When I looked at this list, I didn't feel as scared to turn over control. As many before me have discovered, giving up control to something I trust is not only possible, it can feel like a big relief.

It also helped that turning over control was a gradual process. When I used the scientific method to treat my spiritual quest as an experiment, I gathered a lot of data through prayer and meditation before I was willing to cede any control. Even then, it took time to trust and thus give over more and more control. Luckily, I could take as long as I wanted. My addiction recovery sometimes sped the process because I could go so far off track left to my own devices, but even then, the decision to give over control was voluntary. As I became more comfortable or more desperate, depending on the day, I turned over more and more control, and my life got better and better. If you think it over, that's not such a bad deal.

Feeling Upset With the State of the World

Some people don't connect spiritually because they feel upset at the conflict and cruelty of this world. In my experience, this is based on the preconception that spirituality necessitates a deity, usually one who is all-powerful and thus to blame for either allowing or creating all that trouble. To make matters worse, such a deity often was initially presented as a kind and all-loving god, so the letdown of seeing terrible things happen is that much greater.

The person who rejects spirituality on this basis is really rejecting one particular religious conception without realizing that there are an infinite number of possible variations of spirituality. Many of these don't require them to accept any deity, especially one who seems incompetent, negligent, uncaring, or downright cruel. In essence, this brand of spiritual rejection runs into the same problem as the atheist's argument discussed earlier: it is really objecting to a particular religious idea rather than the much broader field of spirituality.

If this issue is part of your spiritual struggle, I'll tell you what worked for me. I decided at a certain point that I don't need an interventionist god. What I could really use is a higher power that guides me. One way I express this is to say that I don't need a higher power that gets me a better parking spot, I need one that helps me deal with the parking spot I find. This sidesteps the whole issue of thinking, "If there is a god in charge, why are they doing such a terrible job?"

Another helpful idea is to think that if there is a spiritual force that does guide the affairs of the universe, then it is so for beyond me that I am never going to get why it does what it does. Even if its motives are completely in line with mine, its methods may still leave me baffled.

In considering this, it helps me to think of the dogs I've had. I wanted them all to have great lives, and some of the money I earned provided them with food and shelter. There was no way to explain this to my dogs, so they were disappointed when I left them behind to go to work. They were also not thrilled when I kept them from running freely around the neighborhood or helping themselves to food off the table. They nonetheless trusted me as much as they could and followed my directions most of the time.

If it was out of reach to explain why I was leaving when I went to work, it would have been even more of a stretch to explain what I did when I was there, let alone how that connected to their food and shelter. Such concepts are beyond a dog's possible understanding. If you can accept that all this is true, imagine how much greater the intellectual gap between me and any being or force that manages the affairs of the universe. I have to accept that such a higher power's actions are way beyond my comprehension, while still conceiving of its intentions as being good and loving.

I could also expect that a higher power can see further ahead than I can, just as I could see further ahead than my dogs. When I don't like something that is happening now, I might reassure myself that my higher power is planning something good. Perhaps that good is not directly for me but may benefit future generations. If I accept that this is possible, then today's discomfort does not sting so much. With this in mind, I can follow the directions of my higher power most of the time, just like my dogs.

Depression and Hopelessness

While depression and hopelessness seem to interact with spirituality, the connection between them is poorly understood. A recent study showed that the connection between spirituality, religion, and depression is more complex than usually assumed. Spirituality and religion are usually associated with lower levels of depression over time but this can vary by age group (less effect for younger people), cause of depression (spirituality helps more for people with chronic psychiatric issues, less for people with chronic physical illness), varies in sometimes unexpected ways (less depression for people of low or high spirituality and religion, but little effect for those with moderate spirituality and religion), and has negative associations in some cases (more depression for those who report spiritual struggle).[18] Most importantly, it is hard to tell which one is cause, which one is effect, or whether there is another factor that is determining both. This leaves a number of questions for which there is not yet a good answer. Does spirituality lead to less depression, or does the depression determine how spiritual someone will be? Do they influence each other in an upward or downward spiral? Is there another factor, such as genetics, that significantly influences both how depressed and how spiritual someone is likely to become?

It is particularly worthy of note that in about half of the studies reviewed, the association of spirituality and depression is not very strong, although this may be because every study has a slightly different definition of spirituality, and the studies vary on what aspects they are examining.

When 138 studies on this subject were reviewed, 49% showed significant association.[12] The strongest association was between regular spiritual and religious participation and a decrease in depression over time. Thus, getting involved in a regular spiritual practice or attendance of religious services may give you a chance of lowering or warding off depression, and this may in turn make it easier to connect with spirituality, but we can't be absolutely sure. The best we can say is that it can't hurt, especially since regular spiritual activity can lead to a greater overall sense of connection, which is associated with many psychological and practical benefits.

If you feel strongly that your depression is getting in the way of spirituality, I recommend addressing the depression head-on while also trying to get involved in regular spiritual or religious practice even if it doesn't feel like it is doing much for you at first. For the depression, get into therapy, exercise regularly even though you don't feel like it, and see a medical professional in case there is an organic component. Even if none of these things makes you into a spiritual guru, they have really good odds of making your life better, and that's why you showed up for all this, right?

While I'm lucky that depression and hopelessness are not usually my issues, my wife has struggled with these things for as long as I've known her, which is over three decades as of this writing. She has nonetheless often been a more spiritual person than me. At this point, I would call her the most spiritual atheist I know. How does she do it? One of her best tricks is to use a broad definition of spirituality. She does not get into any religion, but instead leans upon the worldwide energy of people who are successfully using the same recovery principles that work for her. In other words, she allows herself to feel connected to millions of people at the same time even though she hasn't met most of them. She regularly fellowships with some of them through meetings in person and online, talks almost every day with others who are improving their lives, and prays without defining to whom she is praying, if it is anyone at all. She just knows that saying the prayers helps her. She regularly reads inspirational writings from those who have done similar work to improve themselves.

If depression is a major issue for you, I hope her example inspires you. It has certainly inspired me.

Genetics and Spirituality

While the genetics of spirituality have not been studied as extensively as some of the other things in this chapter, what research I could find all agrees that there is a genetic association with spirituality. In short, certain genetics seem to help determine a person's chance of being spiritual.[5]

For instance, genetic variations influence the production of various neurotransmitters, which are the chemicals your brain uses to create your thoughts and feelings. Making and absorbing more or less of a given neurotransmitter can have a profound effect on your experience of life, your feelings, and your behaviors.

Let's look at a few neurotransmitters that are involved in spirituality. Your genes influence how much you create and absorb oxytocin, which has been associated with our sense of connection and social bonding, among other things.[5] Since these factors are a major part of spirituality for many people, someone with more oxytocin production will have a greater chance of being more naturally spiritual. Similarly, your genes will influence how much serotonin you produce. Increased levels of serotonin will give you greater openness to experience and feelings of self-transcendence, two traits associated with spirituality. It is also notable that serotonin production and spirituality both hit peak levels in adolescence,[5] a time of spiritual exploration and questioning for a lot of people. This does not guarantee causality, but it does make me wonder. Finally, the neurotransmitter dopamine is a brain chemical strongly associated with motivation and pleasure. Genetic variations that cause less dopamine to be available or absorbed lead to less spirituality and more self-destructive behavior, such as addiction. In contrast, higher concentrations of dopamine receptors seem to go with greater openness to spiritual acceptance.[5]

On a larger scale, there are a number of brain structures that are associated with greater or lesser spiritual experience. Our Theory of Mind network, which includes parts of the frontal cortex and temporal lobes, influences our feelings about prayer and whether there is a personal deity. Our Default Mode network, which includes parts of the cingulate cortex and temporal cortex, influences mystical experiences and self-transcendence, and our temporal lobes in particular are associated with spiritual visions.[6]

We all have variations in our brains, and the parameters of those variations are set by our genetics. Just like some people are born with a greater tendency to be optimistic or mathematical, some of us are born with a greater tendency to engage in and be good at spirituality. We may find spiritual and religious matters to be more rewarding than the average, and thus these behaviors are reinforced, or we may find that they do less for us and are thus internally discouraged.

If you are reading this book, it may be easy to assume you are in the second group. If this is true, don't give up or use it as an excuse. Remember that correlation is not causation The connections discussed above are not as simple as "if you have the wrong genes, you will be less spiritual." Instead, genes give us tendency and potential, as opposed to being fate. This seems especially true of <u>genes that influence behavior</u>. Such genes nudge or even push us in certain behavioral directions, but they can also be profoundly influenced by our environment and experiences.

Think of our brain structures like muscles. If we put them to work, they get stronger; if we neglect them, they get weaker. In our brains, this looks like having more connections and influence for structures that we use more, and less for the parts we don't regularly exercise. For instance, it's been shown that meditation can lead to higher dopamine levels, so regular meditation practice can exercise the parts of the brain that are involved, and the extra dopamine can lead to a greater sense of reward in doing so. If it doesn't come naturally and easily, that doesn't put it out of reach. It just means you may have to work harder to get the gains, but they are there for you.

This was the case for me. Just as I am not a naturally muscular guy, I am not a naturally spiritual guy either. In both areas, I have found that regular workouts make a big difference. I have also seen that I can draw on other tendencies that come naturally to bolster the ones that don't. In the case of my spirituality, I used my natural perseverance to push through when it didn't seem like my spiritual practice was doing much, until eventually I started seeing results. Sometimes these gains were subtle and snuck up on me, like when I noticed that I wasn't a bothered by things not going my way because I had gained a sense that my higher power would help me to be okay no matter what happened. I also used my natural courage to face my fears that I wouldn't be able to feel that spiritual connection that others described, or that there was no higher power there for me.

Find some of your strengths and see how they can help you overcome the areas where you may not be as naturally blessed. You and I may not give the spiritual leaders of the world a run for their money, but we can get a lot better than we are, and thus enjoy the spiritual benefits that are within our reach.

Chapter Four

Some Common Definitions and Perspectives on Spirituality

There are so many definitions and perspectives about spirituality that many people wonder if any of us are even talking about the same thing. Nonetheless, I think it will be worthwhile to go over some of the most common terms and viewpoints. I won't even try to be totally comprehensive, but I'll give the definitions that I think will be most helpful. Thus, in this chapter we will look at theism, atheism, agnosticism, and spiritual-but-not-religious [SBNR]. Following this, I'll discuss how to make these concepts work for you.

Theism

Theism is defined as <u>*the certainty that there is a god or gods*</u>. While this does not have to be associated with religion, in most people's minds, it is. Theism has two major stances, one in which the believer says, "I am certain about the existence a specific god or gods," and the other saying, "I don't know all the details, but there is definitely a god or gods."

Before we get too deep into definitions of theism, however, we first need to define the words "god" or "deity." I use the two terms interchangeably in this section, but for simplicity, I'll just say "god" here. On the most basic level, most people define a god as a higher type of divine or supernatural being, and in the case of monotheistic beliefs, either the only one or the highest in the divine order.[1] Many also think of a god as the source of moral certainty and guidance, i.e., a god is the being that tells us what it right or wrong. Another way of defining a god is that he/she/it is a being that is worthy of worship. These definitions can be mixed and matched. For instance, a god of mischief could be seen as a divine being, while not being a source of useful guidance or a worthy object of worship. That being said, most theists today see their god as having all three aspects at once: divine, a source of guidance, and worthy of worship. With that established, let's look at our two definitions of theism.

The first definition of theism, in which the believer feels sure about a specific deity, is the most common. This is usually associated with a given religion or system of belief. To be sure, it is quite possible for someone to believe in a specific god or gods and argue for this belief, yet not be connected to any religion. This is rarer by far, however, than the number of people who are under the umbrella of a shared faith. For instance, a recent survey in the United States found that about 70% of adults affiliated themselves with a religion, and over 90% of these with Christianity.[2] In fact, for a long time, the term "theism" was considered specific to the Abrahamic faiths, and sometimes used only to denote variations of Christian belief. Few people who study the subject would define it that narrowly today, though.

I gave this type of theism a shot as a young adult, but I found it difficult to sustain. I enjoyed being part of the group worship and diligently studied the same religious text as everyone around me, but I couldn't help but wonder how we all knew for sure that this book was "the truth," especially since there are a lot of other spiritual and religious texts that made the same claim. Nonetheless, I did my best to be a theist of the old-school variety. It just didn't stick very well. While I chose to go straight from this strict theism to an equally strict atheism, it turns out that those weren't my only two options. I might have tried a more inclusive theism, as we'll see next.

This second variation is one in which the theist feels certain there is a god or gods but is less certain about that god's exact identity. This leaves a lot of room for various types of belief, some of which overlap with agnosticism and SBNR, which we will discuss later in this chapter. For instance, this broader theism includes people who have been raised in a religion, no longer subscribe to it, yet still like the basic idea of a higher power. It also includes agnostics who might be surprised to hear that they can also be theists if they believe in a higher power while also thinking that no one can be certain what it is.

I could count myself among their number. I have resigned from the debating society as to exactly what my higher power is but feel certain that there is something on my side. Depending on what definition of "deity" you accept, I might be considered a "soft" theist. After all, I am certain that I have a higher power that is a source of good guidance. I don't concern myself with whether my higher power is, strictly speaking, a "being," so I might not fit perfectly, but I get more from the experience when I talk to my higher power as if I am talking to a friend. If this is an area where you struggle, perhaps this type of "soft theism" might help you, too.

Some theists have a different problem, though. Belief in a deity does not equate to a feeling of connection with that deity. Therefore, some people who feel certain that there is a god and want to feel connected, still don't. They participate in all the rituals and profess all the beliefs, but they don't experience the spirituality that others describe. They compare what they don't feel on the inside to what others seem to feel on the outside. This is a classic fallacy, and as a result, they might feel frustration or even despair in their state of "religious but not spiritual." If this is you, take hope. You are not alone in this, and the suggestions in this book should work just as well for you as for someone who starts without any religious background at all.

Atheism

Atheism has several definitions, the most common being *the certainty that there are no gods or deities of any kind*.[1] A second one is *thinking that the question of a god or gods is inherently meaningless.* A third definition is *a lack of consideration for the question and feeling no need to deal with it.*[1] All of these can be seen as mirror images of theism, so atheism and theism are usually presented diametric opposites.

Since most people think of atheism as an adamant belief in the non-existence of any deity, we will look at this first. This type of atheism can be seen as a belief within itself, rather than a non-belief, since it can be very difficult to prove that something like a god doesn't exist. As mentioned before, this type of atheism seems to most often be in opposition to one particular religious idea or another. For instance, in countries in which the Abrahamic faiths are dominant, atheists are likely to have a bone to pick with those religions rather than, say, Hinduism. They are quick to point out what they see as inherent contradictions in the beliefs and hypocrisy in the believers. The prejudice and violence committed in the name of these religions, and often between them, comes up in almost any discussion. The contrast that the atheist sees between stated beliefs and real-world outcomes will be pointed out. Rarely will an atheist talk about the problems with the dominant religious beliefs of some other society. In fact, most atheists don't consider such things.[1] This is a real time-saver, because there are so many religious beliefs and spiritual systems that a die-hard atheist could spend a lifetime trying to refute all of them. Even if they managed to do so, someone would come up with something new and the atheist would have to get to work proving that the new idea is not true.

I had years in my life in which I fit this model of atheism. I did not take into account the almost inexhaustible supply of religious and spiritual concepts and beliefs. I mostly just argued against Christianity because that was almost the only belief that had caught my attention. In fact, I had little argument with Judaism, which was a distant second in my local community. I had almost no awareness of other faiths that might be practiced or at least believed around me. Were there Buddhists? Muslims? Hindus? SBNR? If I think about it, they were all represented, most of them among my friends, but I wasn't gunning for them. Like a lot of atheists, I had a favorite target: the main religion in my area. Like a lot of dominant forces in society, it gets blamed for all kinds of ills, with varying degrees of justification. As far as I can recall, I

Some Common Definitions and Perspectives on Spirituality

didn't even notice this consciously, let alone consider that it didn't make for very philosophically sound atheism. I also didn't consider that there are other ways to be an atheist.

For instance, the next variation of atheism says that the whole question of whether any deity or deities exist is not valid. If the last definition can be summarized as, "There is definitely no god or gods," then this version is more along the lines of, "There is no point in asking if there are any gods." A subset of this is the idea that, "Even if there were gods, there are none worthy of worship." This type of atheism is probably the least common, but it is still worth noting.

Some people take this stance because it sidesteps a lot of the usual religious arguments. Alternatively, it can be seen as a way to push the battle lines of the debate further into enemy territory. Instead of having to argue for the existence of their god, a theist would have to first establish that the question is meaningful. Although many people consider the question of whether there is a god or gods to be the most important question there is,[1] this brand of atheism challenges that proposition, and thus redefines the whole debate.

Speaking of redefining things, there is one more definition of atheism, and it is the one that invites the most people into its tent. This is the state of not believing that there is a god or gods. This way of looking at things includes all the other ideas and then goes on to add anyone who doesn't think much about it, and even those who think a lot about it but can't bring themselves to believe. An example of the latter could be a religious person who practices diligently but cannot find faith in their hearts, or it could be someone who isn't religious but wants to find that spiritual spark that seems to elude them. Either of these might be called "unwilling atheist." As an interesting aside, some philosophers argue that this definition of atheism is so broad that it inadvertently includes other animals and inanimate objects, but I will politely disagree since we can't know for certain what other animals and inanimate objects believe.

While this definition of atheism may seem weird to some people, I include it because it encompasses a lot of the target audience for this book. This is in part because I am hoping to reach people like me, and I spent a good chunk of my life being this kind of atheist. I didn't give the question of a higher power much thought. I understood that other people believed, some of whom I really respected, but I had little interest in joining them.

In my most earnest attempt at religion, I'm not sure I really believed anything being preached, and yet this somehow didn't trouble me much. I wanted a sense of connection but tried to get it from the religious group rather than the god they worshipped. Years later, when I became convinced that developing a spiritual life would be the key to

Some Common Definitions and Perspectives on Spirituality

beating my addiction, I became someone who wanted to have faith but could not wish it into existence. I thus found myself joining the ranks of the unwilling atheists.

If you relate to this, then I hope you are able to find answers that work for you, as I did. In my case, this involved overcoming my fears of being wrong, looking foolish, or choosing the wrong team. While I partly got past these things due to my even greater fear of not being able to stay sober, a spiritual life cannot be sustained on fear alone. Instead, I had to add hope, however gradually. As I did so, I started feeling more and more that there might be a spirituality that could work for me. I no longer cared if this got me membership into anything. I just wanted to feel better. If this was possible for me, I know it is possible for you.

Can you remain an atheist and be spiritual? Absolutely. Spirituality does not require belief in a deity, only a sense of connection to something greater than yourself. This might be the collective energy of a group of people moving toward a higher purpose, the love within all of humanity, the electromagnetic energy that binds all the atoms in the universe together, the vast universe itself, or the Force. It could be the sense of connection you feel when looking up at the stars on a clear night or when standing at the edge of the ocean. Whatever it is for you, it is this connection that matters most, not whether your beliefs match anyone else's.

Agnosticism

Agnosticism is the belief that _it is not possible to have certainty about a higher power_. This could mean that only the agnostic person can't be certain, or in a broader version, that no one at all can be certain.[1] A variant definition of agnosticism is a belief in deities with a simultaneous belief that nobody can know their true nature. As you might imagine, these stances describe a fair number of people. A recent poll estimates that about 5% of American adults, or about 13 million, identify as agnostic,[3] so if one or more of the descriptors above fits you, you are far from alone.

Let's look at the first idea, which is that the agnostic personally doesn't have knowledge of whether either theism or atheism is correct and does not believe they could be offered convincing proof. Like some forms of atheism, this can be seen as a definitive belief in a lack, but it is not a deity that the agnostic thinks is lacking. They may instead believe that their brains don't have the capacity to comprehend or be certain about a deity. Alternatively, they may believe that no evidence could ever be sufficient to prove any spiritual or religious ideas correct. Either way, the point is that they cannot know for sure.

The second type of agnosticism, which includes the first type as a subset, says that no one can be certain about a deity, even if they think they are. It thus implies that people

Some Common Definitions and Perspectives on Spirituality

who claim either theism or atheism are overconfident, fooling themselves, or haven't looked clearly enough to see that they can't see clearly.

For some agnostics, however, it's not really about whether religious or spiritual ideas can be proved. Instead, claiming agnosticism is a handy way to sidestep or deflect religious arguments. Agnosticism takes away the reason for everything from people knocking on doors looking for converts to wars based in religion. Needless to say, such a position does not actually stop all religious debate in its tracks. Sometimes it just changes the nature of the argument.

Many agnostics have yet another reason for this stance. They embrace agnosticism because it leads them to a spirituality that they can accept. This includes those who are okay with the general idea of a higher power but don't like any of the god concepts they have heard. Like atheists, most agnostics have not explored or even considered all the ideas out there, but instead reject certainty about the ones most local and/or known to them. Be that as it may, agnosticism offers a way for them to keep their options open while still getting the benefits of a spiritual life.

The third kind of agnosticism, which concedes the strong possibility of a deity while denying that absolute certainty can be had about his/her/its nature, works well for those who desire spirituality and want a target for their prayers, but don't want to be tied to any given concept. It also does well for those who can't stop chasing their own tails with internal debate about whether they have the "right" understanding of a god or other higher power.

Like "soft" theism, this type of agnosticism describes me pretty accurately. As I mentioned above, it turns out that I can be both a type of theist ("I believe I have a higher power") and a kind of agnostic ("I don't know for sure what it is and I don't think I ever will") at the same time. Not only does this work very well for me, but it is also much better than the running debate I used to have in my head. I had many stretches of my spiritual life in which I would change my mind about where I was getting my guidance from at least five times per day. It isn't that I looked to five different sources. I simply couldn't agree with myself about where the small still voice in my heart was coming from, or where I got my flashes of inspiration. Was it a deity? Was the right side of my brain talking to the left side? Was it a natural intuition that had been there all along but which I had been drowning out? Was I just fooling myself into feeling better? Was this all somehow true at the same time? My type of softly theistic agnosticism allows me to live an amazing life without plaguing myself with such questions. Perhaps it can do the same for you.

Some Common Definitions and Perspectives on Spirituality

Spiritual But Not Religious

The final perspective on spirituality is "Spiritual but not Religious" [SBNR]. Unlike the other perspectives in this chapter, this is not a belief about the existence of deities or what can be known about them. Instead, it is a stance that *it is not necessary to have organization around spirituality or to believe what anyone else believes.*

Among those who identify as SBNR, there is a very wide variety of beliefs, much more than might be found among the adherents of any given faith, even accounting for how much variation can happen within a religion. What SBNR people share is that they believe in something and often engage in some sort of spiritual practice, yet deliberately eschew any organized religion.

SBNR has become one of the fastest growing categories in First World societies.[4] This likely reflects an overall trend in the developed world in which the number of people who identify as religious is dropping while the number of those who say they are "spiritual, but not religious" is increasing. For instance, SBNR now makes up as many as 1 in 3 people recently surveyed in North America and Europe.[5] This trend is not as present in other parts of the world, although some researchers attribute this as much to the difference in birthrates as the importance of beliefs.[5]

Someone who identifies as SBNR may come to this stance as a result of dropping out of a given religion, perhaps one in which they were raised, but still connecting with spirituality. Alternatively, it could come from a sense that there is more to life that what advertising offers yet feeling like organized religion does not appeal. It could be the solution for a die-hard atheist who finds they need spirituality to get through an addiction or other serious life problem.

Whatever the inspiration, SBNR offers a middle path for many people between not believing anything and going all-in on someone else's ideology. It can also be seen as a way of folding spirituality into atheism or agnosticism. For some people, it is simply a way to avoid labels. The term "SBNR" also makes a fun conversation starter when filling out any form that asks for a preferred religion.

As you've no doubt figured out by now, SBNR is a good descriptor of my spiritual stance. While I can see myself in each category of spiritual perspective covered in this chapter, SBNR is the overarching theme. I was unfamiliar with this as a distinct category when I set out to write this book. It was just an expression that I and others around me used. Now, I can see it as a way of thinking about spirituality that puts me in good company with millions of others who are charting their own spiritual course.

How to Make These Ideas Work for You

Each of the four stances described in this chapter is presented as a way to consider your spirituality. They are not signs to hang around your neck or identities you must embrace. Instead, think of each as a philosophical perspective that may serve you in your search for a spiritualty that fits. Consider each one with an open mind to see if it has anything to offer you.

You can try one out for size, walk around the store for a bit to see if you like it, decide if it feels comfortable, and then either put it back on the shelf or take it home to make it yours. Any decision you make need not be permanent, but if you find that one of the perspectives is a good fit, explore it further and take all it has to offer, especially if it helps you feel more comfortable on your spiritual journey

Theism, atheism, agnosticism, and SBNR each have books dedicated to them, websites and social media that can connect you to others who think in similar ways, and scientific papers written about them. A few of these are listed in the References section of this book, which can serve as a starting point. If you feel inspired to explore further, you have a rich journey ahead of you.

Chapter Five

Making Spirituality Work for You

Now that we have looked at the benefits of spirituality, what gets in the way, how to overcome it, and clarified some terms, it's time to create a spiritual practice that works for you. Luckily, there is a wealth of knowledge out there about how to do this. Therefore, what I'm presenting here is a very basic overview along with some practical ideas. To that end, we will look at finding a higher power that works for you, prayer, meditation, how to tell spiritual guidance from self-will, benefits of group spirituality, how to establish a spiritual routine, and the importance of patience and persistence.

Finding a Higher Power That Works for You

The concept of a higher power is central to my approach to making spirituality work for you. It gives you a focus for spiritual practice and a way to frame your spirituality. Before you protest, let's make sure we are talking about the same thing. For our purposes, let's define a higher power as *that which you feel is greater than yourself*. This is deliberately very broad and comes from my definition of spirituality itself. It allows your higher power to be literally anything you want as long as it meets the basic criteria. It need not be a deity or spiritual being, and it doesn't have to resemble anyone else's. This section will help you find a higher power concept that you can wrap your head around and which will get you the benefits of spirituality.

If you feel unsure about where to start, here are a few ideas that have helped others: the spirit of the universe, the wisdom and guidance of past spiritual masters, the life force and connection of everything on Earth, any deity from any religion, loving kindness, the combined wisdom and energy of everyone who is recovering from addiction, your highest self, the ocean, an unnamed spiritual being or entity, all of nature, all of your ancestors, and the small still voice within. For extra fun, keep in mind that you don't have to make a lifelong choice. You can start with one idea and then refine it or swap it out for something else if it isn't working for you.

Some higher power concepts will be more useful to you than others. For instance, choosing a higher power who doesn't care about you or doesn't assist you in any meaningful way will not be very helpful. Despite this, many people have just such a conception in mind when they say "God." I thus advocate for a few basic guidelines when choosing your higher power, or if you prefer, your understanding of your higher power.

I can already hear a few people saying, "Wait a minute. How can I just pick out the qualities I want in a higher power? That seems like making something up or creating my own fairy tale." In response, I will contend that we all do that to some extent anyway, as we'll see below. Most of us just do it unconsciously, basing it on our experiences and things we've been told. Rather than this, make a conscious choice and thus allow yourself to have an understanding that works for you rather than causing you more problems.

For instance, I've seen a lot of people unconsciously decide that their higher power has qualities reminiscent of their parents, especially their fathers. This is even more true if they have a higher power concept based in any religion that presents its deity as a father figure. If their father was angry and unpredictable, they think of their higher power as being this way, too. If dad was gone a lot and aloof when home, they think of their higher power as not being too involved in their lives. Was dad a loving and attentive parent? Then they feel their higher power cares about them and will protect them. The parallels are not always so obvious, but if you write out the ideas you have of a higher power and compare this to a list of your parents' traits, you can see how much of your higher power concept is based on one or both of your parents.

This makes a lot of sense if you think about it. Our parents were our original higher power(s). They were the first things we felt connection with, they were the source of our survival, and they largely had control over our lives. As we grew up, they were our first experience of authority. They modeled stability, or its lack, in relationships. Thus, when we first conceive of a higher power, it is likely that we will draw on these experiences. Unfortunately, our parents may not have been great role models for some of these things, no matter how hard they tried.

As an example, when I was an infant, I got the impression that I could not count on my caregivers for safety and stability. This was never their intention, but it was my takeaway nonetheless. Thus, when someone presented me with the idea of "God the Father," I was not tempted by that offer. No matter how often I was told that I could count on God, I had different ideas. When I later saw that I could benefit greatly by incorporating a higher power into my life, I had to come up with something that was not modeled on my childhood experiences. This involved first acknowledging the influence those experiences had on me. Once I had done that, I participated in healing work to let some of it go, and I found I could conceive of a higher power that would always be there for me.

I was able to do this in part because I realized that if there is a force in the universe that runs the show, or that created everything, or that has the power to make anything happen in my life, or that can just offer helpful guidance that is better than what my conscious mind comes up with on its own, then I am not going to understand that force perfectly.

Accepting this means that whether I intend to or not, I am going to come up with my own understanding. I am reassured in this by also realizing that everyone who sits together in a religious service will nonetheless have their own understanding of the higher power of their faith, even if they are singing and chanting in unison, or reading out of the same text. Each of those people will make conscious or unconscious decisions about which parts of their religion are most important to them, and which qualities of their higher power are the focus. If that is true of religious adherents, isn't it even more likely to be true for someone who subscribes to no particular faith?

Seeing this, I gave myself permission to make a list of higher power qualities that I wanted, and then claim the higher power it described as my own. Now I urge you to give yourself this same permission. You are free to choose whatever qualities you want in a higher power and declare that this is the spiritual force to which you will turn. If you discover on your journey that you need to add or change some of the qualities on your list, feel free to do so at any time. Review your list periodically to both remind yourself of what is on your side, and to make sure it is up to date with your needs.

To give an example, here is my list:

- Loving
- Caring
- Personal to me
- Compassionate
- Wise
- Understanding
- Forgiving
- Helpful
- Creative
- Humorous
- Capable
- Powerful
- Always available
- Bigger than all my problems combined
- Able and willing to keep me sober

- Has better ideas than mine
- More than enough
- Incapable of abandoning me
- Loves me just as I am

The first three things on my list are ones I find particularly essential: *loving, caring,* and *personal*. Loving, because human beings thrive when they feel loved, and I suggest a higher power that helps you thrive. Caring, because if your higher power doesn't care about you, then you aren't likely to feel much support. Personal, because your higher power concept is yours, and a personal higher power is more likely to feel like it's there for you in a loving and caring way.

Now it is time to write out your own list of the qualities you want in your higher power. Don't worry if it seems silly or unrealistic. The simple act of doing this will be a step toward creating a higher power concept that works for you. Once you have the list, you can ascribe these qualities to the deity of a religion, seek out an established god concept that already fits the list, or simply decide that while you don't know for sure what your higher power is, you will only accept something that has those qualities. Thus, when you pray, you might say, "I am only talking to anything that fits my list; anyone else can kindly move along." When I did this, it led to the wonderful and useful relationship with my higher power that I still enjoy today.

This brings us to the next thing on our list of spiritual tools: prayer.

Prayer

The simplest definition of prayer is *the act of speaking or otherwise reaching out to your higher power*. It is practiced in a countless variety of forms throughout the world and in every religion.[1] There are many ways to classify prayer, but I find it comes in a couple of major types: petitionary prayer and praising prayer.

Petitionary prayer is asking something of your higher power. This could be practically anything: healing for a sick family member, victory in battle, blessing for anyone or anything, consecration of a marriage, guidance in a difficult decision, general direction throughout your day, for your ex to die in a flaming car wreck, or literally any other thing you think your higher power could provide.

The effectiveness of prayer in influencing outside events is a subject of much scientific and philosophical debate, including debate about whether it should even be studied.[2] Both the study and the debate have been going on since at least the late 19th Century, when some of the earliest known research looked at the relative life expectancy of people thought most likely to be the recipients of prayer for wellbeing: royalty, children of clergy, and ships carrying missionaries. When comparing these groups to their closest contemporaries (lords, children of other professionals, and other passenger ships), the study found that the groups of people assumed to receive more prayer all died earlier and in greater numbers.[3] Later studies showed that praying for people to have better health and medical outcomes gets mixed results at best, and many researchers conclude that it doesn't really make a difference. Some argue that this is a pointless field of study anyway because people will probably not change their prayer behavior no matter what the scientific research shows.[4]

This is a good point. Let's remember that the spiritual part of the brain is not the logical part of the brain. Thus, people may not be praying for someone else based on a strong belief that it will make a difference in the outcome. Instead, they may pray because it helps them feel better for having done it. They may pray because "it can't hurt." They may pray because it feels better than doing nothing and facing the idea that they have no control over the outcome. They may pray because it leaves them feeling more connected to the person for whom they pray. They may pray because it helps them hold onto hope. They may pray because it helps them feel closer to their higher power. These are all valid reasons to pray, and none of them relies on proof that they will get what they are asking for.

These reasons also highlight that while prayer may not do much to help others, it is more demonstrably able to the help the person who prays. For instance, praying has been shown to help lower blood pressure, heart rate, and breathing, while improving mental functioning and pain tolerance, all in real time as the person prays.[5] An analysis of multiple studies showed that students who pray do better in school.[6] Prayer improves treatment outcomes for alcohol and other drugs when used in Twelve Step recovery models.[7]

One interesting finding is that the type of prayer and religion of the person praying does not seem to make a difference in outcomes. Christians[11] and Muslims[12] both showed improved mental health outcomes when praying in their faith traditions. Similar results have been found for Jain and Hindu prayer,[13] as well as for Buddhist mindfulness practice.[14] Just reading an Islamic prayer to patients in a majority Muslim country and asking them to think about its meaning reduced pain and improved mental health.[15]

I couldn't find any studies that examined how effective it was to for someone of one faith to pray in the style of another religion. If anyone out there has the time, money, and inclination to find out, I'd love to know the results.

It should be noted that in some situations, prayer can be detrimental. If the person praying has a negative or fraught relationship with their faith or their higher power, then it can worsen their mental health.[8] This seems to be most prevalent for people who think their higher power judges them or those who feel disapproval or rejection from their religion. This highlights the importance of establishing and praying to a higher power that loves you in a nonjudgmental way.

One area in which both scientific research and personal experience show good and practical results is in asking for direction. For instance, a study of various prayer practices in Islam showed that the only ones with significant effect were prayers for guidance and reminders of the presence of Allah.[9] Prayer that centers on getting direction from a higher power has been shown to help people with addiction not only recover more effectively, but it also increases their self-esteem and sense of spirituality, while decreasing their psychological distress.[10]

There are not a lot of studies that specifically examine the effectiveness of praying for direction, but the research so far is promising. To this, I can add a good deal of personal and professional experience showing that such prayer is effective both in reducing stress and in getting the guidance it seeks.

I have seen this demonstrated in both dramatic and subtle ways over the past 20 years. When I first entered addiction recovery, I wanted nothing to do with spirituality. Over time, it became apparent that I was struggling to maintain continuous sobriety and wasn't feeling the serenity that so many others talked about in meetings. It was at this point that I started to become open to spiritual practice, with daily prayer as the centerpiece of my efforts. At first, I knew I was being stupid and talking to no one, but I didn't like my alternatives any better so gave I it a serious try. So many people had told me it had worked for them that I was encouraged to stick with it even though I didn't feel anything at first. Over time, the answers started to come.

At first it was all guesswork. "Is this what you want me to do? Is that?" As I continued praying for guidance, I started to notice that certain actions felt or sounded right in a way that others did not.

I still had questions. Was this the voice of my higher power? Was it a natural intuition that I was tuning into for the first time? Was the act of prayer calming my mind enough to hear my "gut instinct?" Did it matter?

All I could say for sure is that I was starting to get direction. I felt very uncertain about it at first, but my confidence grew through the repeated experience of getting better outcomes and feelings. Today, I wouldn't want to move through the world without it.

How do I know I'm getting higher power direction? Sometimes it feels like a tug inside. Sometimes it comes through something I read or hear. Sometimes it is a flash of inspiration. Sometimes I see a kind of picture in my mind of the next right thing to do. As I have practiced following the guidance I receive, I seem to get more of it or at least notice it more. Given how our brains like to reinforce patterns that are working for us, this is not surprising.

I want to be clear that every prayer session is not a deep and meaningful experience with clear answers. There are days that it feels routine, perhaps a little rote, and not much comes to me. Other times, I stop and really think about the words I am saying and listen for answers. On the days that inspiration seems scarce, I keep going, knowing that it is as much the consistency of practice as anything else that gets good results.

In many ways, it is like exercising my muscles. When I set out to get in better shape, it took some time before I saw any difference. I had some faith because I had seen others get what they wanted from structured exercise, but it had not been a regular part of my life for a long time. I sometimes enjoyed the workouts and other times it felt like a chore. Nonetheless, I stuck with it. As it has gotten me what I wanted, it might be tempting to get complacent and quit. I have kept going, though, because I like how I feel when I maintain my exercise routine. Whether each exercise session feels great or not, I know that the cumulative effect is what I am after.

In the same way, I stick with prayer even when it doesn't feel exciting or show immediate results. If I am patient with it, I feel happier, less worried, and more peaceful about my future.

Having looked at petitionary prayer, let's talk about other major category: praising prayer. By this, I mean any prayer that involves worship or gratitude towards a higher power. This might include songs of praise, religious or spiritual dance, recitation of a mantra, poems talking about the goodness of a deity, repeating the name of a deity over and over, or someone in addiction recovery thanking their higher power for another day sober. It could be argued that some praising prayer may have a petitionary intent if the praise is offered in hopes that the higher power will bestow favor in return. For our purposes, this concern can be set aside. Even when it is true, it will not affect the outcomes of engaging in praise.

This is because it is hard to prove intent when people engage in praising prayer and there is no real evidence that having a mixed motive will get in the way. Truth be told, it is hard to find much research that specifically addresses praising prayer, and that which exists is not of the highest quality.[15] Nonetheless, what scientific evidence we have suggests that praising prayer such as spiritual singing or dancing can improve mental health.[16]

We can study it indirectly, however, by breaking praising prayer down into its constituent elements and looking at their known benefits. Most praising prayer seems to be an expression of admiration, awe, gratitude, or some combination of these emotions. There is research showing that awe has benefits for both individual and society, including more life-satisfaction, greater sense of meaning, and increased prosocial behavior.[17] Similarly, admiration can contribute to greater resilience, improved relationships, and even better physical health.[18] There is an even greater body of scientific literature that sings the praises of gratitude. Known benefits include strengthened relationships and social bonds, increased sense of meaning and happiness, better quality of life, decreased psychological distress, greater sense of wellbeing, less chance of burnout, and reduced stress.[19]

When we take all of this into account, it seems clear that praising prayer has great potential to improve your life.

In my own prayer practice, prayers of praise are a major component. I am not bothered if I do not have a strong idea of who or what I am thanking. What matters is that I am grateful for the things in my life in which I see benefit or towards which I feel admiration or awe. This turns my mind towards what I appreciate, especially if it isn't a direct result of my actions. For extra credit, I can give thanks for those natural gifts I possess. It is easy for me to take such things for granted but since I didn't choose to have them, gratitude is warranted. If I want to get really deep, I can give thanks for the challenges in my life and the people who I would not choose to have in it. I may not enjoy them, but they can teach me when I am open to it. Anytime I give thanks, however large or small, it makes my life better.

Some Ideas on How to Pray

So, if you have been convinced that prayer is beneficial and you want to try it, how do you go about it? As you might expect, there are many options. Some of these include repeating a mantra, performing a benediction, speaking freely to your higher power, chanting, singing a song of worship, reciting a pre-written prayer, burning a sacrifice, saying ritual words every time you are in a given circumstance, dancing ecstatically, or saying a quiet "help" or "thanks" in your mind.

Sometimes prayer involves objects and tools, such as prayer beads, sacred garments, candles, a book of prayer, a public or private altar, a singing bowl, a prayer wheel, one or more crystals, or anything else that helps enhance the experience, signals that this is a time of prayer, or acts as a reminder of some kind. There may be certain settings that seem conducive, such as a forest clearing, a place of worship, a shrine, the path to a holy site, or a quiet spot you have created in your living space.

There is no right or wrong way to go about it, and no set time and place that applies for everyone. Prayer can be incorporated into alone time with your higher power, it can be done as part of a group in which each person is praying their own prayers simultaneously, it can be recited together as part of a regular religious gathering, and it can be said in unison with thousands of others at a convention. You might engage in any of these at different times.

What matters most is that you find and do whatever resonates for you. I started with kneeling by my bed right when I got up in the morning and then doing it again right before I went to sleep at night. I most often asked for help, and then gradually started giving thanks as well. I was raised in a cultural tradition in which this was the basic model, so doing it this way probably had some unconscious significance.

Since those early days of my prayer practice, I have expanded my repertoire. I learned a few set prayers that are not specific to any religion, finding that the simplest ones work best for me. My current favorite prayer is, "Show me what you want me to do and give me the strength to do it. Thank you, thank you, thank you." As you can see, this combines petitionary and praising prayer. I also participate in a group chat with several others to whom I feel connected in recovery. Every day, we each post three things for which we are grateful, with a guiding principle that we never repeat anything from any previous post. In doing so, we are all participating in a kind of group prayer. Sometimes I request direction or give thanks silently in my heart throughout my day. I pray in unison at my recovery meetings, and I sometimes write out prayers in my journal.

This writing most often takes the form of two-way prayer, which I find to be a great help in discerning what my higher power wants me to do. It is a written form of prayer originated in 1939, which comes with built-in answers.[20] To try it out, choose a quiet time and place, then think of a question or dilemma in your life. Next, write it out as though you are corresponding with your higher power. Meditate on the question for anything from a few seconds to a minute or two. When you feel ready, write a term of endearment, such as "Dear Child" or "Beloved," and then let the answer flow through you in the voice of your higher power.

I find that this works best if I don't try to figure out what I think my higher power "would say," but instead just let the ideas or thoughts come. If I don't have a specific question or worry to deal with, I just write the term of endearment and then follow it with something my higher power wants me to know today.

Two-way prayer can be customized. You might try praying at different times of day or in different settings to see when and where the words flow most easily for you. You might put on meditative music. You might try reading something you find inspirational beforehand, to see how it feels for you. You might try different terms of endearment to see if one or another resonates more or inspires more helpful messages.

If you start to question whether you are just telling yourself something you want to hear, consider your list of higher power qualities. Are the answers you are getting consistent with the qualities on your list? Do they encourage those qualities in you? If so, you are probably on the right track.

Since two-way prayer notably involves a form of meditation, it makes a perfect bridge into our next aspect of practical spirituality.

Meditation

If prayer is talking to your higher power, then meditation is listening for a response. Any good relationship involves both talking and listening, so if you want a good relationship with your higher power, consider making meditation a part of your spiritual practice.

What is meditation, exactly? Some common ideas include clearing, focusing, or relaxing the mind, and/or thinking deeply about something. Throughout history, meditation has often had spiritual connotations, but many modern people practice meditation without considering this aspect.

There is much research extolling the benefits of meditation. Doing it daily for a few weeks has been shown to improve mood, emotional regulation, attention, and memory even in people who have never meditated before.[21] It leads to better brain function and more grey matter in older adults who regularly meditate.[22] Meditation decreases anxiety, depression, and stress in both the short- and long-term.[23] Additionally, it leads to significant improvements in heart rate, breathing rate, and blood pressure.[24] Meditation can improve recovery from PTSD.[25] It has also been shown to have significant benefits for addiction recovery.[26]

It is notable that in every study, these benefits came after weeks of daily meditation, so keeping it up is a necessary part of the process. There's a reason they call it a "meditation practice."

So, how do you go about it? There is perhaps an even greater variety of forms of meditation than there is of prayer, and that is saying a lot. Meditation can be highly individualized or follow a set of instructions. It is often done while seated but can be practiced while standing, walking, or lying down instead. Some people incorporate meditation into their yoga practice. It can be done silently or using a chanted mantra. It may be focused on mindfulness, a calming scene, or visualizing something you want in your life. It may be done with eyes closed or gazing at an object, a beautiful scene in nature, or the center of a flame. It may be enhanced with relaxing or ethereal music. It may be free-form or guided. It may be done in solitude or with an in-person or online meditation group. These are but a few ideas.

There are no real limitations, so I'll just give three of my favorite meditations here and then point you towards some helpful resources for further exploration.

Our first meditation is a mindfulness meditation. Mindfulness is originally a Buddhist idea that encapsulates both focused awareness and complete acceptance of what you find with that awareness. This acceptance does not mean that you have to agree with everything in your awareness or that you cannot take action. It refers instead to letting go of fear, anger, worry, etc., about what you observe. You can then make decisions based on your core values and strengths rather than being driven by your negative emotions. In this sense, mindfulness involves deepening wisdom. As we will see, it can also be a gateway to deepening spirituality.

In this meditation, you will sit still and try to experience everything your senses can detect, letting any other thoughts come and go. To begin, focus on your breath. Without needing to control it, pay attention to every aspect of your breathing. Feel the air coming in; feel the air releasing.

Notice how it feels in your nose or mouth. Let yourself be aware of the sensation of it in your throat. Feel it in your chest. Notice your body moving with the rhythm of your breath. Let this be the center of your attention.

As distractions and thoughts present themselves, let yourself notice them without judgment and then let them go. There is no need to fight them or push them away. Instead, think of them as clouds drifting across the sky, and then bring your attention back to your breath. As this becomes easier, let your attention spread to the rest of your body. Notice where you are relaxed and where there is any unnecessary tension. With each breath, allow more and more of that tension to melt away, so that you are sinking deeper and deeper into a state of relaxation.

<u>Notice any sensory information</u> and do your best to accept it exactly as it is without judgment. Feel where you are sitting. Notice your clothing and how it feels. Feel the tips of your fingers. Feel your toes. Notice how you feel in your face, especially around your eyes and jaw. If you notice any tension, let it go. Feel your throat. If it feels closed or tense, let it open and relax. Check your heart. Check your belly. As you experience each of these areas in your body, let it relax and soften. Hear the sounds around you without attaching yourself to any of them. Smell any smells in the air. Notice anything you can taste.

See how long you can sustain this. When your notice your attention wandering, gently bring it back to the center of your breath and your accepting awareness. Once you have recentered, see how long you can sustain it from there.

As you try this, be gentle and patient with yourself. There is no perfection to be had here. Instead, complete awareness and acceptance are ideals for you to pursue. The closer you get, the better the results, but no one lives in that headspace all the time.

When first starting out, try sustaining attention to your breath for 10 seconds, then 30 seconds, then one minute at a time. As it gets easier, see if you can go a little longer, then a little longer. Over time, it will get easier, and you may notice that you can drop into a state of mindfulness in more and more circumstances.

For the purposes of discovering or increasing spirituality, mindfulness meditation can be a great way to connect with your higher power. As you find and sustain mindfulness, let yourself be aware of any guidance that may come to you. This could be as simple as a single word, or it might be a complex thought or idea. It may come as a picture in your mind that embodies the solution to a problem that has been troubling you, or it could be an intuition that guides you to the next right action.

Some people find it helpful to record themselves reading through this or any of the other meditation techniques, thus creating their own guided meditation that they can play back while they close their eyes. If you choose to do this, try to use a gentle tone of voice and pause for a few seconds between sentences so that when you listen to it, you have time to take in each instruction and then put it into practice.

You may also find it helpful to keep a journal nearby so that after your meditation, you can write down notes about anything you received. This not only helps you to remember what you got in that meditation, it also allows you to look back over time and see all the messages that have come to you.

Someone told me recently that they lay in bed reading through everything in their meditation journal and thought, "When I see this all at once, it is clear that these messages aren't coming from me. There is a higher power in my life that wants what's best for me." Whether you agree with this sentiment or not, it is hard to deny that this is a beneficial practice. Perhaps you conceive of your higher power as an intuitive wisdom, an inner guide, or your highest self. Tapping into any of these things through meditation and journaling is a great idea, so have no fear that you will miss out on the perks of this spiritual practice just because your higher power is not verifiably something outside of yourself.

The second meditation technique involves focusing deeply on one of the aspects of your higher power list. Consult your list and pick out an attribute, such as love or kindness. Once you have chosen this, move into focusing on your breath, as in the previous meditation. After centering yourself in this way for a minute or two, bring the higher power attribute you chose to mind and focus on it. This might look like noticing all the areas in your life in which that higher power quality shows up, such as focusing on kindness by thinking of any kind people you know and times you have seen people be kind. You might think about how you have been kind and how you would like to be kind in the future. You might think of public or historical figures who have demonstrated or embodied kindness. You might envision yourself surrounded by everyone throughout history and those alive today who have been kind. Feel their energy surround you, bask in it, and see how you can take it on as your own. After you have concluded your meditation, journal about the experience.

The third meditation technique starts with the same centering breathing. Once this has been established, and you are feeling yourself to relax more and more, allow an image to come to mind of a perfectly safe place. It can be someplace you have been before, someplace you would like to visit someday, or a place completely from your imagination. Once you have this image in mind, allow it to come into central focus until you can see it all around you in your mind's eye. Take in the little details and then see it all as one whole. Allow yourself to smell the smells. Hear the sounds. Feel the physical sensations of your safe place, such as the temperature of the air on your skin and what you are wearing.

Take a few moments to notice how it feels emotionally to be in your safe place. Notice especially any positive emotions associated with being there. Now, allow an image to form of a wise guide who joins you in that safe place. This could look like anyone or anything you like, real or imagined. Thank them for showing up, and then ask what message they carry for you today. Listen to what they have to tell you, or perhaps show you. Take it in, and then ask any questions you may have. Listen to their answers without judgment, knowing that whatever they say is a gift for you. Once you have received all you need for now, realizing that your wise guide is available to you at any time, thank them for coming and talking to you, and then let them be on their way.

Once again, look all around your safe place, taking in the sights, smells, sounds, and sensations. Notice whatever positive emotions you are feeling now. Let those positive feelings flow into your heart, filling it up to overflowing, and then spreading throughout your body until your whole being is filled to overflowing with those positive feelings.

After you have taken all you need from this, allow yourself to realize that this safe place is within you and that these positive feelings flow from your own heart, so both are accessible to you at any time. Knowing this to be true, slowly bring your attention back to where your body is sitting. Hear the sounds around you, feel the physical sensations of your body, and then when you feel ready, slowly open your eyes and gently allow yourself to come all the way back. Take a few moments to soak in all you received today, and then journal about your experience and any messages you received through it.

These meditations are but three of an almost endless number, and I encourage you to explore until you find what works for you. As promised, here are a few ideas that may help you in your explorations. There are many recordings of guided meditations available online and more are being added every day. You can get meditation apps for your phone, computer, or tablet. I regularly participate in an online meditation-and-affirmation meeting that brings together people in any kind of recovery from all over the world for 30 minutes every morning. I'm sure it is not the only one of its kind.

There are many books on meditation. My current favorite is "How God Changes Your Brain" by Andrew Newberg and Mark Waldman In it, the authors set out to explore the science of spirituality and they come to the conclusion that meditation is the surest path to the benefits of spirituality. The book includes an entire chapter containing meditation after meditation, with references to scientific studies that show how the various meditations are good for achieving something useful for the practitioner.

If you want to get further into it, there are meditation classes and individual meditation teachers. Some spiritual paths, such as Buddhism or Transcendental Meditation can involve hours of meditation each day, although they do not require so much from most people, and offer guidance on how to participate in their meditation practices.

Whatever you find that works for you, try to practice it daily. One of the biggest commonalities in the research on meditation is that the benefits come from repeated, usually daily, practice. Some studies even validated that there was a minimum, such as finding that things improved for the participants after eight weeks in a way that had not happened at four weeks. In other words, stick with it, and you will see good results.

How to Tell Spiritual Guidance from Self-Will

Now, we come to one of the great questions of the ages: How can you discern what your higher power wants from you? Are you are getting genuine answers or just telling yourself what you want to hear? As you might imagine, there is no way to be certain. There are, however, some good techniques that can help.

When you receive guidance in your prayer and meditation, revisit your higher power list, and then compare it to the message you are getting. Does the guidance seem to be consistent with the qualities of your higher power? For instance, the Oxford Group, who may be credited with the two-way prayer technique, used their "Four Absolutes" as a litmus test for whatever they received in prayer and meditation. They would ask if what they got was consistent with absolute honesty, purity, unselfishness, and love. If so, they considered it to be from their higher power. Your list may look different than the Oxford Group's, but the idea is the same.

The author Harold Kushner, whose work and outlook I admire, says that his litmus test is whether or not the guidance he receives through prayer challenges him to grow as a person, to live with integrity, to do the difficult but right thing.[28] While this may not always be easy to tell, it can be a powerful standard that brings about spiritual development.

Variations on this might include asking if the guidance will lead you toward being more loving, more kind, or any other quality that you think will help you embody your best self.

Another technique is to see how the guidance you are receiving feels on a gut level. I find that my higher power's will for me seems different in a way that is hard to describe but is often obvious to me. It somehow feels "right," and I know on a deep level that the thing I am thinking or seeing in my mind is what I should do. I want to note that this only started happening after I had been practicing prayer for a while. The basic text of Alcoholics Anonymous puts a lot of stock in seeking intuitive guidance through prayer and meditation. It suggests that when a person first attempts to find such guidance, they may struggle to discern what is coming from their higher power and what is not, even doing some silly things that they mistakenly think their higher power wants from them, but that this "higher power intuition" will eventually become an invaluable resource.[27] I have certainly found that to be true in my life.

I also find that I can hear my higher power's guidance through others. This may come through inspiring readings or directly from other people. Whether these are spiritual leaders, poets, or people in my recovery meetings, I keep my mind open to hear wisdom that feeds my highest self and improves my thinking. This doesn't mean I just go with whatever someone else tells me. Instead, I have cultivated a number of people who comprise my spiritual guidance team. I know I can call them with a dilemma or a harebrained idea and get good feedback. I will ultimately make my own decision and take responsibility for my actions, but this team is a conduit through which I hear my higher power's will, whether they think of themselves in this light or not.

I encourage you to start building your team. Notice who in your life seems to not only give good advice, but who also gives it in a manner that feels consistent with your higher power's qualities, such as giving you feedback with kindness or straightforwardness. Cultivate these relationships by talking to them regularly. Don't talk to them only about your issues but also help them where you can. In this way, you will build a spiritual community of your own, with your higher power at the center.

If all else fails in determining what your higher power wants from you, you can use a process of elimination. When faced with choices about my next move, there are always some things that I feel confident are not what my higher power would guide me to do. For instance, my higher power has never told me to relapse. I've never thought that being unkind to someone is what my higher power wants. I've not been told to lie, cheat, or steal.

Once I have eliminated the obvious no-go ideas, I can apply the other techniques outlined above. Out of the choices that are left, which ones are most consistent with my higher power qualities? Is there any one of them that feels right, or at least more right than the others? Can I take the remaining list to trusted people and get feedback? Doing so may help me pare the possibilities down until my higher power's will becomes more obvious.

As with the other ideas in this book, try each of the above techniques to see what works best for you. They are all things that can lead you to your higher power's will. The more you practice them, the better your results will be.

Group Spirituality

Group spirituality refers to any situation in which two or more people reinforce each other's spirituality by gathering to participate in spiritual activity. This is very important because humans are communal, tribal animals and we are thus built for connection. I believe this underlies our spiritual nature, and it explains why so much spirituality is practiced and strengthened in groups.

Group spirituality includes such things as informal gatherings, religious festivals, group meditation, and regular formalized religious worship. It can take place in almost any setting, although many people associate it most with places designated for this purpose, such as a mosque or a special forest glade.

Just as there are many people for whom spirituality is solely an individual experience, there are many others for whom group spirituality is the only type they know. They may go to a place of worship and sing, pray, and chant in unison with others, but not give this aspect of their lives much thought in between meetings. For others, the social aspect of religious or spiritual gatherings is an important part of their lives, something that binds them to others in their community and helps inform their identity. Many such people will carry the energy and support of their spiritual group with them until the next gathering.

I encourage you to at least try group spirituality. There are too many varieties to name here, so do not be limited by the types you saw growing up or what happens to be common in your area. Instead, explore. I am reminded of the year that my daughter went on a spiritual quest while we lived in Taos, New Mexico. She attended everything she could find, including all the Christian churches in town (she made a fine Virgin Mary in one of their Christmas productions), the Hindu temple, a friend's Bible study, a formal Torah study in Santa Fe, conversations with people who were SBNR, and finally a spiritual home at the Taos Jewish Center. It was this that she liked best, where they discussed readings from the Torah weekly without a rabbi, and the group engaged in passionate debate without needing anyone to be right or wrong. Throughout my daughter's spiritual search, she found some connections, explored identity, cried when her voice wasn't respected and people she loved were maligned by some of the ministers, and eventually found a place she felt she belonged for as long as it served her. She visited many of the groups only once; others she attended for months. Most importantly, through this journey, she learned more about herself and what fit her best.

If you have trouble finding something locally, there are many groups available online or by phone. These forums make group spirituality available to people who would otherwise never find each other. Take advantage of these resources to further your exploration.

It is completely up to you how much group spirituality you add to the mix. I will say that my life has been transformed by the group spirituality I find in both recovery and meditation meetings. They give me a forum in which I can talk freely about my spirituality with like-minded individuals. I hear from others who are further along the path, who have stronger connections to the higher power of their choice, who feel calm about things that cause me stress, and who encourage my spirituality at every turn. I grow by talking with them, hearing their perspectives, and seeing how they approach life in a spiritual way.

I also benefit from seeing people struggle in these meetings, because this tells me I am not alone and that I don't need to be perfect. It also gives me the opportunity to be of service to them and encourage them the same way that has been done for me. When I talk with someone who is struggling or when I share at a meeting, I sometimes hear myself say something that is exactly what I need to hear. I see these moments and messages as gifts from my higher power.

I feel confident in saying that without the regular experience of group spirituality, I would not be writing this book, because I would not be as much of a consciously spiritual person.

Putting Together a Spiritual Routine

Since it usually takes time to achieve the results you want from spirituality, it is important to establish a spiritual routine to keep yourself on track. Like many lifestyle changes, it's better to make small, manageable changes that accumulate over time rather than trying to get it all done at once. While it may be tempting to go on a "spiritual crash diet," this will likely result in finding yourself right back where you started, except a little more discouraged about your ability to have spirituality in your life.

To avoid this, list all the things you want to have in an ideal spiritual practice, but don't try to add them all at once. Instead, pick one thing from your list, and make it a part of your daily routine. Experiment with it to find the way that works best for you. Be open to letting it evolve. Play with it, savor it, notice how it grows and deepens over time. Let it settle in and become yours before adding the next thing from your list.

Consider having a regular time of day for your spiritual routine. I think the first half-hour after waking is the most important in terms of setting the tone for the rest of the day, followed in importance by the last half-hour before bed. Incorporating spirituality into these times can make all the difference.

As an example, I'll share my current morning and evening spiritual routines.

Morning

1. Pray first thing when I roll out of bed, usually a simple request for my higher power's will for me and the power to carry that out.
2. Read something inspirational. Currently, I use two daily readers. I've also used spiritual poetry or a paragraph or two from an inspirational book.
3. Engage in two-way prayer, which includes meditation.
4. Do yoga and a little exercise.
5. Most days, I get on an online or phone recovery meeting. This reinforces the message of living a spiritual life, as that's at the core of these meetings.

6. Engage in creativity. I find I'm most creative in the morning, so I usually take at least a few minutes to be in touch with this.

All of this takes about an hour. When I first started, I was lucky to get five minutes of spirituality into my morning, usually just prayer and nothing else. As I slowly added elements to my routine, I found myself devoting more time to my morning spirituality because each new practice added something to my life. Instead of feeling like my spiritual routine was taking time from other things in my day, I found that everything else I do is enriched by it.

Evening

1. Review my day using a routine set of questions. There are some good suggestions out there for questions you can ask yourself. I use a set from recovery literature, in which I check in to see if there was resentment, selfishness, dishonesty, or fear in my day, consider whether I owe an apology or need to talk about something, check if I was loving toward everyone, look at what I could have done better, and celebrate what went well.
2. Look for three things for which I can be grateful in my day, and then post them to my gratitude group.
3. Pray just before I roll into bed.

Clearly, my evening routine is shorter than my morning routine. This is done deliberately for a couple of reasons. First, if I want to get something done, it works better to make it part of a morning routine than to leave it for later and then find I am too tired, distracted, etc. Almost all my spiritual practices started out as new and not very appealing, so I did them in the morning and that's where they stayed. Second, my evening routine is part of settling in for sleep, so I want it to be gentle and not too full.

Your spiritual routine doesn't need to look like mine, but if you're starting from scratch, look it over for ideas and then pick one thing to try. Keep it up for a while, ideally until it feels like it's yours, a regular part of what you do in your day. Then, look for the next thing you want to add, and then repeat the process of making it yours. If you keep this up, you will wake up one day and find you have a spiritual routine of your own, one that enriches and provides a framework for the life you want to live.

The Importance of Patience and Persistence

The importance of patience and persistence in your spiritual practice cannot be overstated. This is because the kind of spirituality for which I advocate in these pages is not generally found in an "aha" moment or a blinding flash of light that transforms everything. I'm not discounting the power of such experiences, but I can say that they are relatively rare and cannot be gotten by sheer force of will. For instance, some people who have had a near-death experience talk about how much it changed their lives, but I don't think it is a good idea to try to manufacture one. In contrast, patience and persistence in activities like prayer, meditation, and the creation of spiritual community are highly recommended.

I understand that for some of us, these things are less appealing because they don't offer instant satisfaction. Like many changes you can make, they work in part because they take time. This makes them more likely to become a regular part of your life and thus have long-lasting positive effects.

I also understand that it may be difficult to be patient and persistent in spiritual activities when you have little faith that these things will produce results. For some, this is the biggest sticking point of all. If this is the case for you, most of the things in this book are here to help you overcome your doubt enough to at least try.

As I shared earlier, I knew when I started praying that there was nothing there, that I was being foolish, that I was wasting time. This was based partly in my prejudice about religion and partly in an old fear that things that are effective for other people won't work for me. As you've gathered by now, I was wrong on all counts. I have gotten prodigious results from my "prayer experiment," and have since added all the various practices and techniques that are recommended in this book. I suggest them to you because I have seen through personal and professional experience that they work.

Most take regular practice, however. It is easier to start something new than it is to keep it up. Similarly, doing it for a little bit and then giving up is easy, but will land you right back where you started. As they say in some recovery meetings, "If you do what you've always done, you'll get what you've always gotten." They also say that all the suggestions you hear in the meetings come with a "misery-back guarantee." I couldn't agree more.

Try some of the techniques and then stick with them for at least a few months of daily practice. It may be helpful to journal or rate how you feel when you start and then see how those feelings change with time and spiritual effort.

To this end, I've come up with a Spiritual Feeling Scale. Before you add a new spiritual practice, such as prayer or meditation, give each of the following a rating from 0-10, where "0" means "I completely disagree with this statement," and "10" means "I completely agree with this statement."

1. I am a spiritual person.
2. I feel connected to something greater than myself.
3. My life has meaning.

4. Spiritual guidance is available to me.
5. I feel peace in my heart.
6. I feel good about my future.
7. I can handle whatever life throws my way because I am not alone.
8. I intuitively know what to do in stressful situations.
9. There is a higher power that loves me.
10. I feel a sense of purpose in what I do.

Now add up all 10 items, and you will have an overall score between 0-100. Let's call this your Spiritual Feeling Score. Write down both your individual answers and total score, and then put this away for later. Practice your new spiritual technique for a month and then rate each statement and add up the total score again. Compare this to your baseline score. Repeat this process after three months, six months, nine months, and a year of daily practice. This will give you a way to see how each item and your overall score are affected by your spiritual efforts. You may find that some spiritual practices have more impact in your life than others. If so, you can use this information to either experiment and adjust those individual aspects of your practice, or to change the overall balance of your efforts.

Regardless of whether you decide to use the Spiritual Feeling Scale, I strongly suggest picking one or more spiritual practices and sticking with them for some time. The longer you go, the more likely you are to see meaningful results.

Concluding Thoughts and Good Wishes

If you made it this far, you have learned about the many benefits of spirituality, confronted some of the major roadblocks and considered how to get around them, learned the meaning of a few spiritual terms, and looked at ways to put spiritual practices to use in your life.

With all of this, you should have enough to make a good start to having a more spiritual life. If, as the title of this book implies, you hated spirituality when you started out, I hope you have gotten past that prejudice as I did, or at least you hate it a little less.

I am excited for you as you embark on your spiritual journey. I may be more excited than you are right now, but if you stick with it, you will catch up. I believe in you, and I hope we meet along the way.

Love and light,

Casey

Thanks

Thank you to all who have taught me about spirituality and been so patient as I have stumbled through my spiritual journey.

There were early teachers who did their best with me despite the indifference and resistance of my youth. I may not remember your names, but I thank you for trying.

Then there are those who have taught me more recently, through both word and example. Arnold Alderman has been a steadfast mentor and shone a light on the path as he walked ahead of me. David Moretti knows a lot more about this subject than I do, and I am grateful for his companionship and kind feedback. There are the countless people in recovery to whom I owe a debt of gratitude, both those who came before me and those who stand shoulder to shoulder with me now. I would not be here without you.

I am deeply appreciative of everyone who has supported and encouraged me as an author. In particular, Michaela and Chris Kapilla have not only given kind words, but they have also offered ideas, editing, spiritual perspective, and thoughtful feedback. Heather Ingram and Shannon Malish, along with the amazing teams they lead at InMindOut Emotional Wellness Center and Windmill Wellness Ranch, respectively, have been steadfast supporters and examples of how to make dreams happen through serving others.

Above all, there is Kira, always Kira. You opened my eyes to spirituality that could work for me and watched, bemused at times, as I tried various paths and ideas. You have always shown me the spiritual side of things whether I wanted to see it or not, and especially illustrated the power and importance of love as a guiding spiritual principle.

References

Chapter One

1. Willard, A. K., Norenzayan, a. (2017). "Spiritual but not religious": Cognition, schizotypy, and conversion in alternative beliefs. *Cognition, 165,* 137-146.

2. Pew Research Center. (2018). *The age gap in religion around the world.* Retrieved from: https://www.pewforum.org/2018/06/13/why-do levels-of-religious-observance-vary-by-age-and country/

Chapter Two

1. Boniwell, I., & Tunariu, A. D. (2019). *Positive psychology: Theory, research and applications.* London: McGraw-Hill Education (UK).

2. Hoffman, E., Jiang, S., Wang, Y., & Li, M. (2021). Travel as a catalyst of peak experiences among young Chinese adults. *Journal of Humanistic Psychology, 61*(4), 608-628.

3. Mirivel, J. C. (2019). Communication Behaviors That Make a Difference on Well-Being and Happiness. *The Routledge handbook of positive communication: Contributions of an emerging community of research on communication for happiness and social change, 6.* New York: Routledge.

4. Martinez, C. T., & Scott, C. (2014). In search of the meaning of happiness through flow and spirituality. *International Journal of Health, Wellness & Society, 4*(1).

5. Negri, L., Cilia, S., Falautano, M., Grobberio, M., Niccolai, C., Pattini, M., ... & Bassi, M. (2022). Job satisfaction among physicians and nurses involved in the management of multiple sclerosis: The role of happiness and meaning at work. *Neurological Sciences, 43*(3), 1903-1910.

6. Filkowski, M. M., Cochran, R. N., & Haas, B. W. (2016). Altruistic behavior: Mapping responses in the brain. *Neuroscience and Neuroeconomics, 5,* 65.

7. Ostaseski, F. (2013). *Serving others, transforming ourselves.* Retrieved from: https://www.lionsroar.com/serving others-transforming-ourselves/

8. Shattuck, E. C., & Muehlenbein, M. P. (2020). Religiosity/spirituality and physiological markers of health. *Journal of Religion and Health, 59*(2), 1035-1054.

References

9. Moradi, N., Maleki, A., & Zenoozian, S. (2022). The efficacy of integrating spirituality into prenatal care on pregnant women's sleep: A randomized controlled trial. *BioMed Research International, 2022.*

10. Ferreira-Valente, A., Sharma, S., Torres, S., Smothers, Z., Pais-Ribeiro, J., Abbott, J. H., & Jensen, M. P. (2019). Does religiosity/spirituality play a role in function, pain-related beliefs, and coping in patients with chronic pain? A systematic review. *Journal of Religion and Health*, 1-55.

11. Burlacu, A., Artene, B., Nistor, I., Buju, S., Jugrin, D., Mavrichi, I., & Covic, A. (2019). Religiosity, spirituality and quality of life of dialysis patients: A systematic review. *International Urology and Nephrology, 51*(5), 839-850.

12. Villani, D., Sorgente, A., Iannello, P., & Antonietti, A. (2019). The role of spirituality and religiosity in subjective well-being of individuals with different religious status. *Frontiers in Psychology*, 1525.

13. Kao, L. E., Peteet, J. R., & Cook, C. C. H. (2020). Spirituality and mental health., *Journal for the Study of Spirituality, 10* (1). 42-54.

14. Tay P, K, C, Lim K, K. (2020). Psychological resilience as an emergent characteristic for well-being: A pragmatic view. *Gerontology, 66.* 476-483.

15. Vigliotti, V., Taggart, T., Walker, M., Kusmastuti, S., Ransome, Y. (2020). Religion, faith, and spirituality influences on HIV prevention activities: A scoping review. *PLOS ONE 15*(10).

16. Aten, J. D., Smith, W. R., Davis, E. B., Van Tongeren, D. R., Hook, J. N., Davis, D. E., Shannonhouse, L., DeBlaere, C., Ranter, J., O'Grady, K., & Hill, P. C. (2019). The psychological study of religion and spirituality in a disaster context: A systematic review. *Psychological Trauma: Theory, Research, Practice, and Policy, 11*(6), 597–613.

17. Vincensi B. B. (2019). Interconnections: Spirituality, spiritual care, and patient-centered care. *Asia-Pacific Journal of Oncology Nursing, 6*(2), 104–110.

18. Wilkinson, D. J. & Johnson, A. (2021) A systematic review of quantitative studies capturing measures of psychological and mental health for gay and lesbian individuals of faith. *Mental Health, Religion & Culture, 24*(9). 993-1016.

References

19. Hodapp, B., & Zwingmann, C. (2019). Religiosity/spirituality and mental health: A meta analysis of studies from the German-speaking area. Journal of religion and health, 58(6), 1970-1998.

20. Bensaid, B., ben Tahar Machouche, S., & Tekke, M. (2021). An Islamic spiritual alternative to addiction treatment and recovery. *Al-Jami'ah: Journal of Islamic Studies, 59*(1), 127-162.

21. Foster, K. J., & Tzu, L. (2018). 12-Step Spirituality. *Spirituality and religion in counseling: Competency-based strategies for ethical practice* (C. S. Gill & R. R. Freund, Eds.). Routledge.

22. *Alcoholics anonymous big book* (4th ed.). (2002). Alcoholics Anonymous World Services.

23, Zemore, S. E., Lui, C., Mericle, A., Hemberg, J., & Kaskutas, L. A. (2018). A longitudinal study of the comparative efficacy of Women for Sobriety, LifeRing, SMART Recovery, and 12-step groups for those with AUD. *Journal of Substance Abuse Treatment, 88*, 18-26.

24. Beraldo, L., Gil, F., Ventriglio, A., de Andrade, A. G., da Silva, A. G., Torales, J., ... & Castaldelli-Maia, J. M. (et al.) (2019). Spirituality, religiosity and addiction recovery: Current perspectives. *Current Drug Research Reviews Formerly: Current Drug Abuse Reviews, 11*(1), 26-32.

Chapter Three

1. Dictionary.com. (2021). *Skepticism.* Retrieved from: https://www.dictionary.com/browse/skepticism

2. Comesaña, J., Klein, P. (2019). Skepticism. In E. N. Zalta (ed.), *The Stanford encyclopedia of philosophy.* (Winter 2019 Edition). Stanford. Retrieved from: https://plato.stanford.edu/archives/win2019/entries/septicism/

3. Hurtt, R. K. (2010). Development of a scale to measure professional skepticism. *Auditing: A Journal of Practice & Theory, 29*(1). 149–171.

4. Pettit, M. (2021). *Theology.* Retrieved from http://www.muggletonian.org.uk/Theology.html

References

5. Anderson, M. R., Miller, L., Wickramaratne, P., Svob. C., Odgerel, Z., Zhao, R., & Weissman, M. M. (2017). Genetic correlates of spirituality/religion and depression: A study in offspring and grandchildren at high and low familial risk for depression. *Spirituality in Clinical Practice, 4*(1),43-63.

6. Van Elk, M., Aleman, A. (2017). Brain mechanisms in religion and spirituality: An integrative predictive processing framework. *Neuroscience and Biobehavioral Reviews, 73.* 359-378.

7. Ecklund, E. H., Johnson, D. R., Scheitle, C. P., Matthews, K. R. W., & Lewis, S. W. (2016). Religion among scientists in international context: A new study of scientists in eight regions. *Socius: Sociological Research for a Dynamic World.*

8. Campbell, C., & Bauer, S. (2021). Christian Faith and Resilience: Implications for Social Work Practice. *Social Work & Christianity, 48*(1).

9. Chamsi-Pasha, M., & Chamsi-Pasha, H. (2021). A review of the literature on the health benefits of Salat (Islamic prayer). *The Medical journal of Malaysia, 76*(1), 93-97.

10. Timko Olson, E. R., Hansen, M. M., & Vermeesch, A. (2020). Mindfulness and Shinrin-Yoku: Potential for physiological and psychological interventions during uncertain times. *International Journal of Environmental Research and Public Health, 17*(24), 9340.

1. Draper, P. (2017). Atheism and agnosticism. In E. N. Zalta (ed.), *The Stanford encyclopedia of philosophy.* (Winter 2019 Edition). Stanford. Retrieved from: https://plato.stanford.edu/archives/win2019/entries/aheism-agnosticism/

12. Braam, A. W., & Koenig, H. G. (2019). Religion, spirituality and depression in prospective studies: A systematic review. *Journal of Affective Disorders, 257*, 428-438.

Chapter Four

1. Draper, P. (2017). Atheism and agnosticism. In E. N. Zalta (ed.), *The Stanford encyclopedia of philosophy.* (Winter 2019 Edition). Stanford. Retrieved from: https://plato.stanford.edu/archives/win2019/entries/aheism-agnosticism/

References

2. Smith, G. A. (2021). *About three-in-ten U.S. adults are now religiously unaffiliated.* Retrieved from: https://www.pewresearch.org/religion/2021/12/14/abut-three-in-ten-u-s-adults-are-now-religiously unaffiliated/

3. Pew Research Center. (2021). *Measuring religion in Pew Research Center's American trends panel.* Retrieved from: https://www.pewresearch.org/religion/2021/01/14/masuring-religion-in-pew-research-centers-american trends-panel/

4. Willard, A. K., Norenzayan, a. (2017). "Spiritual but not religious": Cognition, schizotypy, and conversion in alternative beliefs. *Cognition, 165,* 137-146.

5. Pew Research Center. (2018). *The age gap in religion around the world.* Retrieved from: https://www.pewforum.org/2018/06/13/why-do levels-of-religious-observance-vary-by-age-and country/

Chapter Five

1. Davison, S. A. (2021). *Petitionary prayer*. Retrieved from: https://plato.stanford.edu/entries/petitionary-prayer/

2. Parks, B. N. (2019). Simon says: On the magical impulse of studies on the efficacy of intercessory prayer. *Christian bioethics: Non-Ecumenical Studies in Medical Morality, 25*(1), 69-85.

3. Halperin, E. C. (2001). Should academic medical centers conduct clinical trials of the efficacy of intercessory prayer?. *Academic Medicine, 76*(8), 791-797.

4. Rosner, F. (1975). The efficacy of prayer: Scientific vs religious evidence. *Journal of Religion and Health, 14*(4), 294-298.

5. Chin, F., Chou, R., Waqas, M., Vakharia, K., Rai, H., Levy, E., & Holmes, D. (2021). Efficacy of prayer in inducing immediate physiological changes: A systematic analysis of objective experiments. *Journal of Complementary and Integrative Medicine, 18*(4), 679-684.

6. Jeynes, W. (2020). A meta-analysis on the relationship between prayer and student outcomes. *Education and Urban Society, 52*(8), 1223-1237.

7. Hai, A. H., Franklin, C., Park, S., DiNitto, D. M., & Aurelio, N. (2019). The efficacy of spiritual/religious interventions for substance use problems: A systematic review and meta-analysis of randomized controlled trials. *Drug and Alcohol Dependence, 202,* 134-148.

8. Braam, A. W., & Koenig, H. G. (2019). Religion, spirituality and depression in prospective studies: A systematic review. *Journal of Affective Disorders, 257,* 428-438.

9. Guldas, F. Z. (2021). Cognitive-behavioral-related prayer types and mental health relations among Muslim samples. *Cumhuriyet İlahiyat Dergisi, 25*(1), 437-454.

10. Hai, A. H., Wigmore, B., Franklin, C., Shorkey, C., von Sternberg, K., Cole Jr, A. H., & DiNitto, D. M. (2021). Efficacy of two-way prayer meditation in improving the psychospiritual well-being of people with substance use disorders: A pilot randomized controlled trial. *Substance Abuse, 42*(4), 832-841.

11. George, K. (2019). *Too blessed to be stressed? Correlations between prayer, scripture readings, and mental health measures* (Doctoral dissertation).

12. Najam, K. S., Khan, R. S., Waheed, A., & Hassan, R. (2019). Impact of Islamic practices on the mental health of Muslims. *International Dental & Medical Journal of Advanced Research, 5*(1), 1-6.

13. Stroope, S., Kent, B. V., Zhang, Y., Spiegelman, D., Kandula, N. R., Schachter, A. B., ... & Shields, A. E. (2022). Mental health and self-rated health among US South Asians: The role of religious group involvement. *Ethnicity & Health, 27*(2), 388-406.

14. Thapaliya, S., Upadhyaya, K. D., Borschmann, R., & Kuppili, P. P. (2018). Mindfulness based interventions for depression and anxiety in Asian population: A systematic review. *Journal of Psychiatrists' Association of Nepal, 7*(1), 10-23.

15. Eilami, O., Moslemirad, M., Naimi, E., Babuei, A., & Rezaei, K. (2019). The effect of religious psychotherapy emphasizing the importance of prayers on mental health and pain in cancer patients. *Journal of Religion and Health, 58*(2), 444-451.

16. Malviya, S., Zupan, B., & Meredith, P. (2022). Evidence of religious/spiritual singing and movement in mental health: A systematic review. *Complementary Therapies in Clinical Practice, 101567.*

17. Arcangeli, M., Sperduti, M., Jacquot, A., Piolino, P., & Dokic, J. (2020). Awe and the experience of the sublime: A complex relationship. *Frontiers in Psychology, 11*, 1340.

18. Van Cappellen, P., Edwards, M. E., & Fredrickson, B. L. (2021). Upward spirals of positive emotions and religious behaviors. *Current Opinion in Psychology, 40*, 92-98.

19. Day, G., Robert, G., & Rafferty, A. M. (2020). Gratitude in health care: A meta-narrative review. *Qualitative Health Research, 30*(14), 2303-2315.

20. Wigmore, B., & Stanford, M. (2017). Two way prayer: a lost tool for practicing the 11th step. *Alcoholism Treatment Quarterly, 35*(1), 71-82.

21. Basso, J. C., McHale, A., Ende, V., Oberlin, D. J., & Suzuki, W. A. (2019). Brief, daily meditation enhances attention, memory, mood, and emotional regulation in non-experienced meditators. *Behavioural Brain Research, 356*, 208-220.

22. Chételat, G., Lutz, A., Arenaza-Urquijo, E., Collette, F., Klimecki, O., & Marchant, N. (2018). Why could meditation practice help promote mental health and well-being in aging?. *Alzheimer's Research & Therapy, 10*(1), 1-4.

23. Totzeck, C., Teismann, T., Hofmann, S. G., von Brachel, R., Pflug, V., Wannemüller, A., & Margraf, J. (2020). Loving-kindness meditation promotes mental health in university students. *Mindfulness, 11*(7), 1623-1631.

24. Mohan, U. P., Kunjiappan, S., Babkiewicz, E., Maszczyk, P., & Arunachalam, S. (2022). Exploring the role of melatonin in meditation on cardiovascular health. *Biointerface Research in Applied Chemistry, 13*(1). 1-18

25. Jayatunge, R. M., & Pokorski, M. (2018). Post-traumatic stress disorder: A review of therapeutic role of meditation interventions. In: Pokorski, M. (ed.) *Respiratory Ailments in Context*, 53-59.

26. Kadri, R., Husain, R., & Omar, S. H. S. (2020). Impact of spiritual meditation on drug addiction recovery and wellbeing: A systematic review. *International Journal of Human and Health Sciences, 4*(4), 237-250.

27. *Alcoholics anonymous big book* (4th ed.). (2002). Alcoholics Anonymous World Services.

28. Kushner, H. S. (2001). *Living a life that matters*. Random House: New York.

Made in the USA
Monee, IL
09 January 2024

51440961R00094